From Gypsy to Jersey
An Adoption Journey

by Yael Adler

Edited by Carla E. Huelsenbeck
and Catherine Gigante-Brown

Cover design by Vinnie Corbo
Interior design by Vinnie Corbo
Author photo by Natalie Brandt

Published by Volossal Publishing
www.volossal.com

Copyright © 2020
ISBN 978-1-7350184-2-3

TABLE OF CONTENTS

This book is dedicated to my parents,
Marcy and Herb Schusterman,
for giving me a wonderful life.

Preface

There comes a time in every adopted person's life when they want to know the answers to some questions. *What drove my birth mother to put me up for adoption? Does she think about me? Do I have a sibling somewhere out there in the world?* In a study of American adolescents, the Search Institute found that 72 percent of adopted adolescents wanted to know why they were adopted, 65 percent wanted to meet their birth parents, and 94 percent wanted to know which birth parent they looked like. (Source: American Adoption Congress)

Some of us spend most of our lives thinking about these questions, while others do not give it much thought. For me, these questions (and more) suddenly became a near-obsession when I hit my 30th birthday. I don't really have any explanation as to why this deep-rooted curiosity to explore my past occurred then, but I am sure it had something to do with me being in the state of reflection that milestone birthdays have a tendency to inspire.

It wasn't as if my adoption was a surprise. I had known about it all of my life. It was something we spoke about openly in my house. But the story was the typical generic one: the living conditions were poor, my biological mother wanted a better life for me, and so that was the reason for my adoption. That response was fine — it was enough to satisfy me all those years growing up — but now, suddenly, I wanted to know more.

I was standing in the kitchen one evening after dinner, drying some pots and pans, when I looked out into our great room and saw my older daughter entertaining my younger one, making silly faces as my husband sat there with them. They were laughing and having fun, and it put a smile on my face. As I looked around at my home and was reminded of all the fantastic people and things I have in my life, I thought to myself, *Wow, how did I get so lucky?*

It made me think of all of the people responsible for my being where I am today. Of course, I thought of my parents, who gave me a wonderful life filled with love and luxuries that some children could only dream of. And I thought of the dedicated attorney who helped children find families to care for them and who led my parents to me. But it also made me realize that this life I am living is due in large part to a choice that someone made for me 28 years ago. That choice was to put me up for adoption at the age of two, in a small village outside of Arad, Romania. If it were not for this decision, my parents would never have had me, and I would not have had this life that I am grateful for every day.

It was when I was cleaning out my mother's co-op, helping her put it up for sale, that I came across a binder with a lot of documents in it, a video, and some photos. It occurred to me that these were all paperwork relating to my adoption, something I had never seen before. The binder contained the court document, medical records, information on my birth mother, whose name and details I knew nothing about, and more. *Interesting, right after I start giving my adoption some serious thought, I come across this? Tell me that is not a sign of some sort!*

Something inside of me knew it was time that I dig into my past to get answers and write a book about it. Well, truthfully, the notion of writing a book didn't happen just then; I had always wanted to write a book about my adoption. Knowing the bits and pieces that I did know, I thought the story was intriguing: the fact that when my parents could not conceive, an ABC *20/20* special on Romanian adoptions led them to a lawyer, who led them to me. And since it all started with *20/20*, I knew I wanted to publish my book in 2020.

So, what is this book really about? It is about having courage. After years of trying to conceive, my parents had the courage to look into adoption to have a family. I found the courage to go to some lengths to uncover so many unknowns about my adoption.

My message to those of you who are adopted is this: don't be afraid to take a risk and explore this part of your life. It may or may not have a happy ending — no one can guarantee that — but the path to getting answers will give you an appreciation for your life now. And it will tell you a lot about yourself.

My message to parents who have adopted or are looking to adopt is this: know that this day will probably come in your child's life and that it is okay. Be supportive. Try not to feel rejected or defensive, thinking that he or she is ungrateful for the life you provided or is unhappy. It is quite the opposite.

I begin this book with my parents, sharing *their* story, because without them I would not be here writing this. My father passed away six years ago, so their story is told from my mother's perspective. I wish my dad could have been a part of this; not a day goes by that I am not thankful for the relationship we had and for him being the best father I could have asked for.

I think that understanding my parents' experience, the timing of my adoption, and all of the people involved will give you an appreciation for my journey of discovery and the steps I took to get answers.

Thank you for taking the time out of your life to read this. I hope that, if nothing else, it inspires you to step back and appreciate your own life's journey, wherever it has taken you.

CHAPTER ONE

Where It All Began

It was right before July 4th weekend in 1974, and my mother was getting ready to go on a blind date. At first, she was furious that her mother, Charlotte, had given out her phone number without her permission. But her parents had no choice. Her father, Saul, had a co-worker whose wife, Suzy, was very persistent. She would call every night in the middle of dinner, and they could not get rid of her. They were finally so disgusted; they just gave her the number.

"I have a great guy for Marcy," she would say.

My mother, an only child, had been living on her own since she could afford to, at age 24. She lived in a studio apartment on Park Avenue and 34th Street in Manhattan, on the fourteenth floor. It was a luxurious building with a doorman and an elevator operator. She was happy to be out of Brooklyn — out of that two-bedroom apartment with the blinding chartreuse kitchen, the color her mother loved but Marcy could not stand. Away from Erasmus Hall High School, where she felt lost in the crammed hallways of more than 3,000 students.

It wasn't all bad memories in Brooklyn. Marcy had fond memories of her childhood: going to museums, where her passion for art began, building wooden World War II airplanes with her father, and watching old western movies on television. One Saturday her father put on some old cowboy boots he hadn't worn in years. They got stuck on his feet, so he was forced to wear them all day until Charlotte came home in the early evening and helped him get the boots off.

Yes, there were good times, but Manhattan is where Marcy always wanted to be.

For college, she went to the School of Visual Arts and then finished her fourth year at New York University. She pursued a career in graphic design that allowed her to afford the $219 a month rent. (Well, technically, she could only afford $200; Saul slipped her the extra $19 each month.) She described the first job she landed as "the most boring job ever" with *Parents Magazine*. "I did mechanical arts. I had to draw all of the lines and borders by hand, since there were no computers at the time."

But Marcy was making a good salary back then, a whopping $9,500 a year. She dated and had relationships but nothing really serious, which I suppose is how she ended up on this blind date.

A handsome tall guy, with dark hair and a mustache, picked her up. Herb wore gray slacks, a light blue open buttoned-down shirt, a navy blazer, and white shoes with no socks. At first glance, my mother was pleased. She was also relieved that he was tall (she is 5'9"). She wore black silk wide-leg slacks with a black tank top and a white linen blazer with low black sandals. My mother was attractive, with her blonde hair, navy blue eyes, and glowing, flawless skin.

They went to see *Pippin* on Broadway. "He took me to a show so he wouldn't have to talk to me in case he didn't like me," she said.

They didn't talk much during the show. It was pretty awkward, as most blind dates are. Afterwards he asked if she was hungry, so she figured that was a good sign. They walked to Club Imus. Over drinks, they talked about their jobs. Herb was vice president of sales and marketing for Revlon, and my mother was a graphic designer. They both came from small Jewish families, although he grew up with an older sister, in a kosher, more observant household. He was nine years older, never went to college, enjoyed being a bachelor and was in no rush to get married. It didn't seem like they had much in common, but the chemistry was there. And they did agree on two things: how pushy Suzy was, and how much they hated blind dates.

They went back to my mother's apartment, and she remembers that they talked for hours. This was definitely the start of something, my mother felt. She told him she was leaving for Fire Island with friends the next morning. Herb thought he was suave when he told her to "call me collect" (since no one had cell phones back then).

The next day, Marcy hailed a cab to Penn Station. She got into the cab, looked down, and found a wallet on the floor without any identification. There was $400 inside. She wasn't about to leave it for the cab driver, so she took it with her to Fire Island. Her friends were there waiting for her, but once she arrived, she got the urge to call Herb to tell him what happened.

"In the cab this morning I found a wallet with a lot of money in it — I think it's a good omen!" she said.

The excitement in her voice was irresistible, and Herb quickly found himself inviting her to spend the rest of the weekend with him. Without much thought, she accepted and left Fire Island to go to his place in Fort Lee, New Jersey. That was the start of their relationship.

My mom waited patiently and five years later, right before her lease was up, he proposed. They were having breakfast at Herb's apartment before getting ready to spend Hanukkah with family at his sister's house. He asked my mother to grab the muenster cheese from the fridge, and there it was: a ring in the middle of the block of cheese. Kind of a strange proposal, if you ask me, but hey — when you've waited for an engagement ring for five years, who cares what the hell it's in!

Four months after their engagement, they were married. My mother moved out of Manhattan to Fort Lee, where they lived in a two-bedroom co-op with a beautiful view of the George Washington Bridge and Manhattan staring back at them. At night, Marcy enjoyed sitting on their terrace and basking in the glow of the city lights across the Hudson River. She had just lost her job at McGraw-Hill, where she was designing children's books. She began doing freelance jobs designing book covers plus working one night a week teaching typography design back at the School of Visual Arts, where she'd attended college.

The First Steps Toward Adoption

Marcy was 32 and Herb was 41 when they got married in 1979. Some of her friends were already "married with children," while others in her circle were still single. Although she didn't really feel pressured into having kids right away, it was something she had always wanted, so they started trying to get pregnant. But after nine months, it just wasn't happening for them.

During this time, my mother was experiencing severe menstrual pain and bled inconsistently, so she went to the doctor, who told her that she had endometriosis and would need to have surgery. She was terrified at the thought of having to get a hysterectomy, which would not allow her to have kids, but thankfully it did not come to that. Instead, at Beth Israel Hospital in New York, my mom had one of her ovaries removed. The doctor assured her that she could still have a successful pregnancy with one ovary, but that it could take another year before they saw any results.

My parents kept trying to get pregnant, but another year went by and my mom needed a dilation and curettage (D&C), a procedure to remove tissue from inside the uterus. Once again, the doctor told them it might take a while to get pregnant afterwards.

Waiting became part of a never-ending cycle that left them childless. My mother was getting discouraged and cried a lot. One after the other, her friends were getting pregnant. She would go to baby showers and wonder why she could not be as lucky as her friends. My mom took every test imaginable; they were all painful and torturous. She told my dad that maybe it was time he got tested. It turned out that their inability to conceive was a combination of the two of them.

"We just felt like a married couple, not a family," she said in retrospect.

One morning my parents had an appointment with Dr. Rubell, a gynecologist and fertility specialist in Manhattan. The two of them went together to see what their options were. It had already been five years of doing tests and taking rounds of medications without any results. Dr. Rubell told them they had one of two options. They could go to Israel or England – countries that were then known for implementing in vitro fertilization (IVF) – or they could adopt.

Dr. Rubell said, "There are so many children out there waiting to be adopted. Once it's your child, it's your child. It doesn't matter who birthed them."

They thought about what the doctor had told them. They knew picking up to travel to a foreign country wasn't feasible with my father's job. And it wasn't like today, where IVF is commonly done. Then they thought about adoption. They were going to such great lengths to get pregnant that they never stopped to think about adopting. Making that decision to adopt was difficult — it meant facing that they couldn't have a child naturally — but the alternative was worse.

They weren't getting any younger. My mother was now 37 and my father, 46; they knew it was time to start researching the adoption process. A friend of my mother's recommended an attorney, Lucille Rosenstock, in Blauvelt, New York, so they scheduled a trip to go meet with her. Lucille told them about a young mother in Texas who was planning to put her newborn up for adoption. It would be another five months until the birth mother was due, but this time there was something worth the wait for Marcy and Herb: a baby.

My mother thought of a newborn. Something she had wanted for so long. She pictured holding that little baby in her arms, with those innocent new-to-the-world eyes staring back at her. Soothing the baby as it cried. Bonding. Becoming a mother.

My parents were happy together, but each night at the dinner table they imagined another place setting. They would pass their second bedroom longing to convert it into a child's room. The apartment was a lonely reminder that their lives were incomplete.

A lot of back-and-forth communication started happening between Lucille and the birth mother's attorney. The holdup was a Texas state law that gave the birth mother a chance to change her decision once the baby was born. And that is what she did. She had a change of heart.

According to Texas Family Code Sec. 161. 103, "Texas adoption laws state that a birth mother must wait at least 48 hours after the birth of her child before she may give her consent to an adoption. It is important that any woman pursuing adoption is comfortable with her decision before signing the consent paperwork, because her consent in Texas is rarely revocable." This is still the law today. (Source: Adoption Network)

Randomly, I called an adoption attorney in Texas I had found online, and she confirmed these details for me. And in a remarkable coincidence, the attorney also shared that she, too, had tried to adopt in Texas but it fell through — not only for the same reason, but also 28 years earlier.

So just like that, Marcy and Herb's dream of becoming parents was shattered. The baby that my mother had pictured in her arms faded, and they were back at square one.

They mourned the child they never had the chance to love and walked around the apartment feeling empty. Now even more time had gotten away from them. *Are we ever going to have a child?* my mother wondered. She had to reach deep inside herself to not give up. She thought of Dr. Rubell, who reminded her of how many children there were in the world who needed a family, and she found the courage to explore other options. In the meantime, they kept trying to conceive and prayed for a miracle.

It was around this time that Marcy learned of an ABC *20/20* special that was going to be airing. Barbara Walters and Hugh Downs had been broadcasting a moving series on the thousands of Romanian orphans who were turned over to state-run orphanages. Part of the series was a famous segment called "Shame of a Nation," which shone a spotlight on the horrific living conditions that the children were exposed to. Many Americans and families all over Europe were already rushing to Romania after hearing about this, in hopes of adopting and saving these children, to give them a better life.

Another segment would be airing that covered private adoptions taking place in Romania, so Marcy and Herb planned to be home that night to watch the program together. Maybe something in it would speak to them. Maybe it could give them hope.

My mother remembers it was March 1991 when they turned on *20/20*. They didn't know it, but what they were about to watch would lead them to me and that void in their life would soon be filled.

Finding the Courage to Act

Their eyes glued to the television screen, my parents saw so many orphans — so many fragile, malnourished children without families, fear in their eyes, not knowing where their lives would end up. The episode included pictures of villages and private homes in Romania, and the impoverished conditions right after the collapse of communism. The program showed beautiful children who needed homes and their parents who couldn't provide for them. It also showed American families who had adopted children and brought them back to the Unites States.

Searching for hours online, I attempted to find the *20/20* episode that my parents watched. I even wrote to ABC's archives department. But I was never able to find it and never received a response.

Marcy and Herb both got chills seeing the children and adoptive parents at the airport embracing one another and ready to start a new life together. It tugged at their heartstrings. *That could be us*, they thought. They wanted to give a child who had nothing, everything.

They were hesitant to adopt from the orphanages, not knowing what illnesses the children could have been exposed to or what traumas the children there could have faced. The thought of those things was daunting to them, and they wanted to try to avoid those issues if possible. They knew immediately that they wanted to try to do a private adoption instead.

At the very end of the program, Barbara Walters told viewers that if they were interested in getting more information, they could call the studio and get the names of some international adoption attorneys. My parents looked at one another in bed that night with hope for the first time in a long time. They knew they had to call and request more information.

My mother slept well that night, knowing she was going to get the name of an attorney who would help them be a family. She was given the name of someone not too far away. Robert Braun was based out of Philadelphia. He is someone who became incredibly instrumental in my life and the lives of so many children and families.

It took courage for my parents to make that phone call. Many people watch a program like that and sure, it moves them, but it usually ends there. They go on with their lives and don't give it another thought. They don't often take that next step to do something about it. My parents did, and I commend them for it.

My mother called Robert every day for a couple of weeks until she heard back from him. She was not giving up now. On the phone, Robert said he would be traveling to Romania soon, but he didn't know if he could take on any more cases.

My mother pleaded with him and begged him for a meeting. He agreed, they set up a time, and my parents drove to Philadelphia. They spoke with him for hours. They told him how badly they were looking for a child to complete their family. And how desperately they needed his help.

Robert told them he was planning his next trip abroad and that he would be in touch. About three weeks later, my parents got a phone call. It was Robert, calling from Romania. He told them that he had just learned of a mother who would be putting her two-year-old girl up for adoption. He was going to send a video in the mail so they could see what the child looked like and where she lived.

"When we got the video, we were overwhelmed with excitement. We didn't know what to expect," my mother recalls. The video began and they saw a beautiful little girl with olive skin, dark brown hair, and a round face. She was wearing a red headscarf with a long-sleeved white shirt and a light blue skirt. Her birth mother was holding her.

My father always wanted a little girl, and as they looked at my face, they knew that I was the missing piece to their family. They called Robert, saying that they wanted to move forward. He told them he would be returning to Romania soon and would get back to them about next steps.

Weeks went by while Marcy and Herb anxiously awaited Robert's call. They waited . . . and waited. Negative thoughts flooded their heads — thoughts that things were going to fall through like they did the time before, in Texas. They did their best to remain optimistic. When they finally heard back from Robert, he told them what he told all of his clients: If they were willing and able to travel to Romania and see the child in person, it would help to move the adoption along more quickly.

This would be advantageous not only because they could get me out of Romania sooner, but also because if they saw me overseas during the adoption process, then I would receive an IR-3 Visa, automatically granting me citizenship upon entering the United States.

My parents did not need much convincing. Robert told them it would likely be on a few days' notice, but he would arrange all of the flights and accommodations for them. My parents were elated and had no objections. They were ready to make the trip as soon as possible.

CHAPTER TWO

At Last We Meet

As with the Texas adoption, my parents once again went through all of the necessary steps: they were fingerprinted, had blood tests done, completed paperwork, found a pediatrician, met with a social worker, got character letters of recommendation...it was all so familiar to them.

Soon, although it seemed like forever, it was time to make the trip to Romania. They flew out of John F. Kennedy (JFK) International Airport into Bucharest on TWA, one of the major airlines at the time. It was an evening flight with one connection, taking a total of about 11 hours.

"We were so nervous, just as you would be giving birth to your first child," my mother said. She cried almost the whole flight.

They landed in Bucharest sometime in the morning, and they were completely and immediately lost. Nothing was translated into English like it is today when you travel to a foreign airport. They did not have the right currency on them, and they were exhausted from the long flight. To make matters worse, they couldn't find the person Robert sent to meet them.

They sat down in a restaurant to get their bearings. I guess they stood out, because it wasn't long before Robert's contact approached them and introduced himself. He escorted them to help find their luggage for their next flight to Arad, which would be another two hours. They landed in an old-fashioned airport where they had to walk down the plane steps and across the tarmac. There, another person who worked for Robert greeted them as they came off the plane.

Her name was Gabby, and she was Robert's right-hand person. She helped him with everything relating to the adoption process. She had short red hair, was dressed casually, and was maybe in her 30s. Gabby spoke English and had a taxi waiting to take them to their hotel.

My mother recalls, "The hotel was like out of a 1950s movie, probably a five-star hotel for that time." It was small and old fashioned, but nice. The lobby had lots of gold and marble. They checked in, then went to freshen up and have a drink. But they couldn't eat anything; their stomachs were in knots.

Their first stop was an apartment building where I was staying with a woman named Lilly. She was what Robert described as a "transitional caretaker." Since I already had lived with my birth mother for two years, it was important to transition me from that home as soon as possible. This was an effort to ensure that the process ran smoothly and that is where Lilly came into the picture. I stayed with her for about a month until I was able to come to the States.

Lilly was kind. She had long dark hair and was in her late 30s. She lived in the apartment with her son and her mother.

It was there that my parents saw me for the first time. It seemed like they had waited a lifetime for this moment and suddenly, here it was. I was no longer someone they dreamed about — I had now come to life. I was in a room with them, where they could hold me and get to know me.

I hid behind Lilly, frightened. In an attempt to break the ice, Lilly suggested maybe going for a walk and getting out of the apartment. There was an aqueduct nearby, so we all went for our first walk together. This was worse. I was even more scared leaving the apartment.

We went back inside, and Lilly gave me a snack. My parents watched me eat some salami and tomatoes, and patiently continued to try and engage with me. They tried to hug me to show some sign of affection, but I refused. I kept yelling "Pee-pee, pee-pee!" They caught on quickly that I didn't really have to go to the bathroom — it was just a clever tactic to get away from them.

They were heartbroken, but they understood that it was going to take time. It was getting late, so my parents said goodbye and Gabby took them back to the hotel. My parents went to dinner, and my mother remembers the restaurant not having any menus — they just served you what they had. She ate foods like stuffed cabbage and beef, and recalls them serving *a lot* of vodka.

Marcy and Herb did not see Robert much during their time in Romania, but Gabby was there to take them around. She met them for breakfast the next morning at the hotel. The server brought over prune jam with an assortment of breads. The breads and cakes were delicious. My mother lived on them while she was in Romania.

After breakfast they all went back to see me at Lilly's apartment. I wasn't as scared during this visit, probably because they brought me clothes and gifts. Smart move, right? My mother remembers me being so skinny that all of the clothes she brought were huge on me. They brought me pink sneakers, jeans, and a lavender-purple stuffed teddy bear, who later on took on the name Purple Berry. They also gave me my first lollipop, which I could not get enough of. I

warmed up to them and actually gave them a smile for the first time, which meant the world to my parents. They stayed for most of the day so that I could become more familiar with them and comfortable with them. They kept to that same schedule for a couple of days so we could continue to bond.

On May 31, 1991, the third morning they

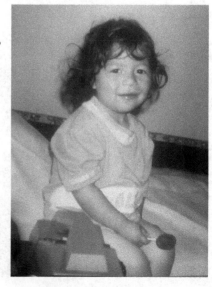

were in Romania, my parents went to the courthouse in Arad to have my adoption legalized. As they approached the *palatul justitiei* (the courthouse) they were nervous. They had waited so long for this moment and it was finally here.

There were quite a few people in the room, including two judges, the district attorney, the court reporter, and a delegate of the Tutelary Authority (Child Protective Services). Also present was Giovanni Martinelli, a man who worked with Robert and appeared in court on his behalf that day to translate.

My parents had brought and offered each of the attendees a pin with both a Romanian flag and an American flag on it, which everyone in the room accepted graciously. My mother said things were brief and to the point. They were asked the typical questions, such as why they wanted to adopt and what type of life they would be providing. They told the court that they could not have children and that they wanted to give a child a wonderful life filled with love and happiness. Things concluded with papers being signed, and just like that the adoption was official. After about ten years of trying to conceive and a previous failed adoption, Marcy and Herb now had a child.

My parents were filled with joy, but it felt surreal at the same time. The waiting had finally come to an end, and their dreams of having a child of their own had now come true. They would now be a family, which is all they ever wanted.

Once things were finalized, my parents decided that they wanted to meet my birth mother. They called Robert and asked if he could set up a meeting. "We wanted to see who the mother was. We wanted to see what the culture was like, what the people were like," my mother explained to me later.

Robert agreed and made the arrangements for them to meet in a park in Arad. As my parents waited for my birth mother to arrive, their bodies tensed up, their hearts were racing. *What if she doesn't like us? Could she change her mind and take our daughter away?* It was pretty nerve-racking.

She finally arrived. They all smiled and shook hands. My birth mother came with a few family members and handed my parents beautiful fresh flowers. My mother said they were told not to bring anything so it wouldn't seem corrupt like some of the other adoptions that were taking place in the country. So, my parents had just brought some American candy bars and coffee — things that my Romanian family would not have access to.

My birth mother was very straight-faced and did not show much emotion, but my mother knew how difficult this decision had to be for her. My parents thanked her and told her that they would take good care of me and give me a wonderful life.

They were not able to take me home with them on that trip, for reasons that are still unclear. Possibly there was a delay with the paperwork at the American Consulate. It was hard for them to leave me behind. It seemed unfair; they finally got the child they had been longing for, but they still had to go back to their empty apartment. There wasn't much they could do — it was out of their hands. But they decided to do something that *was* in their control, so they left an audiocassette tape with their voices on it so that I could listen to it every day for my remaining time in Romania.

My First Journey Home

On June 28, 1991, an employee of Robert's escorted me onto an airplane and flew with me to JFK airport, where my parents and grandparents were waiting for our arrival. I screamed a lot. I had never been in a car before or an airplane. I immediately went to my Grandpa Saul, as if something about him brought me comfort; perhaps he reminded me of someone I knew. He was the only one who was able to calm me down and make me feel safe at that moment. We then climbed into a black limousine and went straight to my new home.

I really hated the car. I screamed the entire time. When we finally arrived home, my mother was excited to take me around and show me the house — especially, my bedroom. They had decorated it for me in beautiful white furniture from Bellini, a high-end children's furniture boutique. It had a bed, which was foreign to me. I was used to sleeping on the floor. I didn't know what a bed was.

That first night they put me in my pajamas to get me ready for bed, all I did was scream. Cookies finally calmed me down. It was an adjustment for everyone, and the next few weeks were hard. I wouldn't sleep in the bed, so my parents finally consulted my pediatrician, Dr. Asnes. He said that if I was more comfortable sleeping on the floor to just let me sleep on the floor. Simple enough. So that is what they did. My parents took turns sleeping in the room with me so I could eventually acclimate and feel safe.

It felt like we were finally starting to get into some kind of routine. One day a friend of my parents who spoke Romanian, among other languages, came to the apartment. My parents were curious about what I was saying and wanted to see if he could pick up on anything. He told them that I was actually speaking two languages: Romanian and some dialect that was probably from my village. Through research for this book, I found out what that dialect was — it was Romani, the spoken language of the Roma people, also known as Gypsies. (We will get into that more deeply later in the book.)

My parents played a lot of Romanian music on cassette tapes and did everything in their power to make me feel special and loved. The car, on the other hand, was still an issue. I couldn't seem to make one trip without screaming the entire time. Luckily, my parents came up with a solution: every time we went out, we made Dairy Queen a required pit stop to put me more at ease. It worked.

Gradually, more and more people learned about me and recognized us as a family. No one knew about my parents adopting until it was finalized. They hadn't wanted to jinx anything. People expressed such happiness for us. Neighbors approached my mother out of the blue and shared their own experiences of adopting and the challenges they had conceiving. My mother said she never felt any judgment or stigma surrounding the adoption.

After a few weeks, I began to quickly adapt. I started catching onto English, and I cried less and less. I had a loving family who had been waiting for me for a long time. I had everything and more. And that is how my life started. A life filled with privileges that would have never existed if I stayed in Romania. It took the courage of my parents to never give up on having what was so important to them — a family.

CHAPTER THREE

Meet Robert Braun

Twenty-eight years later, when telling my mother that I was interested in writing this book, I asked for the full name of the attorney who was involved in my adoption, figuring that would be a good place to start. He was always referred to as "Lawyer Bob" in our household — which obviously is not super helpful when conducting a Google search.

When my mother told me he was Robert Braun of Philadelphia, I did a quick Internet search and found what I thought might be him, based on his background and description. I was able to track down an email address and thought, *What the hell, let me shoot him an email and see what happens.* So, on May 23, 2019, at 2:46 p.m., I crafted an email with the subject line "You Were Involved in My Romanian Adoption." It read:

Hi, Robert.

My name is Yael Adler, and I believe you were the attorney that my family used to adopt me from Romania in the early 1990s. First and foremost, I would like to thank you for being so instrumental in finding me a loving family.

Second, I would like to ask you for a favor. I have decided to write a book on my adoption, and since you were involved in that, I was wondering if

I could include you and have a few moments of your
time. Of course, I do not expect you to remember
me or my parents specifically, given that you helped
many families, but it would be great to get a sense of
what it was like being in your position, connecting
Romanian children with American families right after
the collapse of communism.

I would appreciate any time you could spare.

Thank you,
Yael

I really wasn't expecting much, although of course I did
hope for some type of response. But it was only a few hours
later, in the early evening, that I got a call. I couldn't believe
it, it was him! I had actually found the attorney who was
involved in my adoption 28 years ago and I was speaking to
him on the phone. I was so excited and in complete shock at
the same time. I was trying to hold a conversation, but what
was going through my head was: *Holy shit! I can't believe I
am speaking to THE Robert Braun right now. This can't
be real.*

What it did was give me hope that this book might
actually happen and that I now had a chance, with Robert's
help, to piece together so much of my story that I never
knew. And after speaking with him, it occurred to me that I
knew nothing at all — but I was eager to learn.

Robert and I talked briefly on that initial call, and he was
kind enough to offer his help with my book. He said that he
was a bit tied up for the next two weeks, but after that he
would be free to schedule a phone interview. I thanked him
profusely and started putting together a list of questions in
preparation for our interview.

On the evening of June 13, 2019, we had our first
interview. Robert jokingly warned me that he can be a bit
chatty, and our conversation did take its twists and turns.
But that was fine — all I wanted to do was listen and absorb

whatever it was he had to say so I could learn more about him and his work.

I was truly fascinated with his life story. I told him he should be the one writing a book. But he said he had no interest in writing one. So, here is what I learned about Robert and how he ended up in Romania, a country he became very fond of.

The Evolution of "Lawyer Bob"

Born in 1948, Robert Braun grew up in Brooklyn and was the first kid in his family to go to college. He graduated from high school at age 15 and went on to Brooklyn College. He said his biggest issue was that he excelled at everything and had no desire to do *anything*. In the middle of his senior year, when he was 19, he decided that he didn't want to live at home anymore. With one semester left in college, he dropped out and became a member of VISTA (Volunteers in Service to America).

At Brooklyn College he had been an anthropology and linguistics major. Foreign languages came pretty naturally to him. With that background, he was assigned by VISTA to the Navajo Indian Reservation, which was one of the only placements where you had to learn the native language. So, Robert picked up Navajo, which he said was difficult, and managed to succeed as a community development organizer. Among his supportive roles in the community were working to help Navajos bring electrical wiring to their hogans (traditional Navajo huts made of logs and earth) and counseling unwed mothers and mothers-to-be on how to continue their high school education.

After a year and a half as a VISTA volunteer, Robert came back to finish his degree at Brooklyn College. He then got a full fellowship for graduate school at the University of Illinois to study anthropology, becoming a specialist in the peoples of the Amazonian region.

After graduate school, Robert got a teaching job at Bryn Mawr College, a women's college in Pennsylvania. Why did he choose it? Because he was, *and still is*, a feminist. He genuinely wanted to teach at a place that believed young women should have the same educational opportunities as young men, which, in the 1970s was still a challenge.

It turns out, this job became the pivotal point that led Robert to working in international adoptions.

In the late 1970s, he received a grant from the National Science Foundation that allowed him to take a small group of undergraduates to learn how to conduct anthropological research in the Amazon rainforest. The travel agent who was coordinating the trip called Robert up one day.

"When you're down in Peru, do you think you could do me a favor?"

Robert said, "Yeah sure, what do you need?"

"Can you look around and see what the situation is in Peru about adoption? We have a fertility problem, and we would love to do an international adoption. We don't know how to get started, but maybe you can help us."

It was this random phone conversation that sparked something in Robert. During any downtime in his trip, he did adoption research for the travel agent, and he found the whole venture fascinating. It was then he decided that this is what he should be doing with his life.

A New Calling

Robert resolved to change his career and transition from teaching anthropology to doing adoption work in Latin America. (If you think about it, this is a type of anthropology.) But it occurred to him that he could not make such a drastic career change in just one step, especially without the financial capital to support him. So, he decided to open Andes Art Gallery, which featured various Latin American artists and painters, as well as Latin American folk art that he had collected over the years. Simultaneously, Robert was working as a part-time consultant for the Organization of American States regarding handicraft development, helping indigenous people market and benefit economically from their traditional-crafted products.

After about four years, Robert had enough financial stability to make the move into doing adoption work. But before he could begin, he realized he was missing an important credential that would give him legitimacy in the world of international adoptions: a law degree. So just like that, he went back to school, attending Temple University. Once he got his law degree, in 1984, he started the International Families Licensed Adoption Agency.

Robert hired a few employees in Philadelphia and began doing adoption work in Latin American countries — primarily in Colombia, Peru, Chile, the Dominican Republic, Guatemala, and Mexico.

Blown away by all of this, I asked him, "How did you find people to work with in all of these countries so quickly?"

"I'm very resourceful," he said.

I laughed. "No, but really, tell me how you did it."

Robert said he talked to people; it was as simple as that. He would get recommendations from a pediatrician or lawyer about birth parents who were looking for adoptive parents. Then he would speak to those birth parents to get an intuitive sense of whether he felt comfortable with them and if they felt comfortable putting their child up for adoption with one of his clients.

He made it all sound so easy, even though I am sure it wasn't. The reality was, he was an intellectual and a personable guy. To his advantage, he spoke several languages fluently, and he had a quirky personality which made him easy to talk to and connect with.

As Robert continued to do adoption work, he learned about the political situation in Romania and it piqued his interest. The year 1989 was a significant one. Aside from it being the year I was born (which I like to think is pretty significant), it was also the year of the Romanian Revolution that put an end to communist rule with the execution of dictator Nicolae Ceaușescu and his wife, Elena. It set in motion a chain of events that left an exorbitant number of children available for adoption.

Robert felt like he should go to Romania and scope things out. So, in March 1990, he flew to Romania via Istanbul. On his connecting flight from Istanbul to Bucharest, he sat next to a gentleman named Giovanni Martinelli. They struck up a conversation which led to an enduring friendship. (It was clear to me that Robert had a way with people, so this came as no surprise.) Giovanni ended up being Robert's first representative in Romania and helping in other ways — even occasionally appearing in court in the event that Robert could not be present himself. In fact, that was exactly how Giovanni became involved in my adoption case. Robert asked my parents to sign a power of attorney agreement that would allow Giovanni (in Robert's place) to appear with them in court, where he provided translation on the day of my adoption hearing.

Robert said that Romania became a hotspot for adoption interest because there were so many kids eligible. However, people were a little fearful of Romania because of AIDS and other health concerns that were uncovered, so only a few adoption agencies were starting to work there — and everyone was learning as they went along.

With his experience doing adoptions in many other countries, it did not take Robert long to learn how the adoption system worked in Romania. What was really interesting, he said, was that at the time he did not even need a license there. He was simply a person from America who was a practicing attorney and the director of an adoption agency.

He described his agency as very hands-on. He had his own staff in both Philadelphia and Romania, he spoke Romanian fluently, and he traveled there eight to ten times a year. This allowed him to control every aspect of the adoption process, compared with other agencies that had to rely on sources overseas.

In Romania, Robert visited several orphanages, the judges in family court, Child Protective Services, and the maternity hospitals. He got to know everyone and people enjoyed his company because he was easy to talk to. Even more so, he was likely the first American they had met who visited, spoke their language, and embraced their culture as deeply as he did.

Robert developed many relationships that allowed him to quickly gain recognition. One in particular was with the director of the maternity hospital of Arad, who would let him know when someone was looking to put their newborn up for adoption. Robert said he would sit down to talk with the director, the birth mother, and the hospital social worker to see if the birth mother would feel comfortable giving her child up for adoption and if the birth mother had any terms. For instance, would she only be willing to do the adoption if Robert swore to secrecy, so that no one in her village would find out? Did she want to meet the adoptive parents first? There could be any number of terms or conditions, he said.

The hospital director took great satisfaction in knowing that children could have the opportunity to leave Romania and have a good life, so he enjoyed working with Robert when situations like this arose. Interestingly enough, I was born at that very maternity hospital, but I was not adopted as a newborn.

Robert's Vital Role in My Adoption

I went home with my birth mother and stayed there for another two years before leaving Romania to live in the United States. Now, you might be wondering why she would wait rather than put me up for adoption as a newborn, and I wondered that, too. The decision to put your child up for adoption is difficult enough after bringing her into the world. To take her home and watch her grow and develop, bond with her, watch her first steps, listen to her first words, see her become a person…It baffled me how anyone could give away a child after experiencing all of these significant milestones.

There had to be some logical and compelling explanation. I just did not know what that was, but I knew it was something I wanted to find out.

In Romania, the judge of the family section of the general court system approved all adoption petitions. An adoption petition, Robert explained, is a form that tells the judge about the child being adopted and the parents wishing to adopt. To determine if the adoption was in the best interest of the child, the judge typically asked the adoptive parents why they wanted to adopt as well as why the birth parent or parents were looking to put the child up for adoption. However, the judge was also used to hearing the same answers over and over again, Robert said. Adoptive parents want to fill a void in their life and give a child in need all the love they can possibly give. Biological parents say that they want a better life for their child, a life with more than they can physically provide for them.

These responses were common, so the determining factor in whether or not the judge granted the petition was based on input from someone else — an individual who played a vital role in the adoption process, the delegate of the Tutelary Authority. Robert said the social workers in the Tutelary Authority in every county in Romania were the ones who took care of infants who were at risk physically or legally when no one else was there to take care of them.

"The social worker from the Tutelary Authority was an honorable person who would conduct an investigation and provide a report to the judge in every adoption case," Robert said. "Each report ended with a recommendation as to whether or not he or she felt the adoption was taking place

for the right reasons and in the best interest of the child."
Then the judge would make the final decision.

Following this, the judge's opinion would be rendered
in writing by the judge's secretary and signed by the judge.
Many copies were made for different people, including
everyone involved in the case plus the city hall — in
essence, the civil registry of the jurisdiction where the
case was held and where a new birth certificate would
be produced. Then all the paperwork would go to the
American Consulate.

In my situation, much of the paperwork had been done
in advance since, a few months prior to the court hearing,
my parents had been pre-approved to bring me into the
United States as a statutory orphan. Robert educated me a bit
about form I-600A on the US Citizenship and Immigration
Services (USCIS) website, which is the Application for
Advance Processing of an Orphan Petition. People can get
pre-approved to bring an orphan into the United States
from any country by filling out this application and having
a home study done by an adoption agency that is licensed
in the state where they live. The home study would include
things like fingerprinting, background checks, and letters
of recommendation.

Since my parents were living in New Jersey, a New
Jersey-licensed agency performed the home study and sent
it to Robert's agency in Philadelphia. The study was then
translated into Romanian and given to the Tutelary Authority
and the judge.

At the time of my adoption, there were not as many
strict procedures in place as there are now. Romania was still
in shambles, and an adoption could happen pretty quickly.
Robert told me that he had cases where adoptive parents
came to the country, met the child they were adopting, and
then went home with their child, all in a week's time.

It wasn't until a few years later that the adoption process
became more layered, requiring more intensive involvement
of local Child Protective Services and more communication

on a local and national level among different parties before even reaching the court. In the mid-1990s, private adoptions completely stopped, and families mainly adopted from the orphanages directly. The restrictions became tighter and tighter until international adoptions were eventually banned. Today, adoptions out of Romania to the United States have resumed, but there are a number of strict requirements. (Source: U.S. Department of State - Bureau of Consular Affairs website)

This all made me think about timing — how everything happens when it is meant to happen. My family was so fortunate that everything happened when it did, and we will always have Robert to thank for that. It was his competence and his passion for bringing families together, and for finding children a safe and caring home, that made my story possible.

Robert has retired from doing adoptions but still works, running an Airbnb in Philadelphia and operating a fingerprinting business as well. He told me that he intentionally left his email available online so that anyone he may have worked with in the past would be able to find him. From time to time, people whose cases he was involved in — people just like me — reach out to him for help in discovering their roots.

Robert and I had planned to meet right before COVID-19 broke out in 2020. The virus that seemed so far away, originating in Wuhan, China, suddenly appeared in the United States, then in my backyard and all around us. While our face-to-face meeting has been delayed, we continue to communicate by telephone.

In the meantime, I hope Robert still gets satisfaction from knowing that he helped to make so many lives better. Including mine.

CHAPTER FOUR

The Backdrop – Communist Romania

Understanding what it was like in communist Romania and understanding post-communism is vital to understanding my adoption story. Robert was kind enough to connect me with a woman who worked with him and grew up in Romania during the 1980s and 1990s. He said she would be a good source to speak to — someone who could paint a vivid picture of what life was like back then, to provide context. Out of respect for her privacy, I am going to give her a fictional name. Let's just call her Alexandra.

In the late 1980s, Alexandra was 17 and living in communist Romania under the dictatorship of Nicolae Ceaușescu. Her family was more privileged than most, living in central Bucharest where there were more resources than surrounding areas. Her mother worked as an administrator in a Romanian child protection governmental office, while her father was an engineer. Still, things were scarce.

Her father made a decent salary, but there was not much they could buy with the money he earned. There was no food. "You would go to the grocery store and there would be two items on the shelf: mustard and champagne," Alexandra recalled. Surrounding areas had even less.

Romania had a large foreign debt that needed to be paid off, so Ceaușescu basically exported all of the country's resources: food, fuel, medicine, and more. That left

Romanians with essentially nothing to live on, making it nearly impossible to put food on the table and provide for a family.

Even for those who were "well off," times were so desperate that people would randomly form lines outside stores in hopes that someone might arrive with food. Alexandra vividly remembers her and her family taking turns waiting in line for hours. If they were lucky and someone showed up with food, the whole family would come back to try to get as much as they could. But they were also on a meal plan, so there were per-person limits on whatever little food there was. Even bread was rationed.

In 1988 and 1989, the government routinely shut off the electricity, so people would only have limited power, which would include television. During the hours of 6:00 p.m. to 8:00 p.m., television would show what the leader had done that day, five minutes of Romanian cartoons to say goodnight to the kids, and the rest would be propaganda. Alexandra said that every Saturday night, week after week, everyone watched the same show, *Dallas*, which (ironically) was about a wealthy dynasty. It was the highlight of everyone's Saturday, she said.

Alexandra remembers attending a school where, during the winter months, there was no heat. She would keep her coat and mittens on all day. Even today, living in the United States and holding a prestigious position at an Ivy League school on the East Coast, she keeps the temperature warm in her house at all times. "I lived through enough cold nights in communist Romania, I can't do it anymore — it brings back too many bad memories," she told me.

Since Ceaușescu wanted Romania to operate similarly to communist North Korea, his mission became to produce more communist citizens. To increase the birth rate and the overall population, women were forbidden from having any access to contraceptives or from having an abortion. If anyone performed an abortion or knew of someone getting one, they would all go to jail — the woman, the abortionist, and anyone who knew about it.

Women were getting pregnant left and right, with no resources available to provide for their children. Many were living in constant fear and would go to all sorts of extremes to try to abort on their own, such as taking large doses of pills or using coat hangers. Many of them died.

Countless children were being abandoned or turned over to orphanages. The result: there were hundreds of thousands of children in Romanian orphanages in the 1980s and 1990s. This is not to say that all of these children were unwanted or that their birth mothers or parents were being cruel, Alexandra said. People simply had nothing to give and probably thought their children might be better off in an orphanage.

What time revealed was that these orphanages did *not* take good care of these children at all. In 1990 when ABC's *20/20* began broadcasting its series on Romania's abandoned children and the orphanages, word started getting out about the brutal living conditions in these facilities. Children were getting sick and dying due to the lack of sanitation and improper care. This was the reason many families in the United States, Europe, and surrounding countries flooded Romania to save these children and adopt them.

Speaking From Experience

Alexandra became pregnant at age 17 and was among the many Romanians who did not know what to do. In an effort to keep it from her parents, she initially confided in a close friend. That friend gave her pills to take on an empty stomach in an attempt to abort the baby. She took increasing doses of the pills to see if that would work. It didn't.

What happened next was to be expected. Alexandra became extremely ill from the pills and had episodes of severe vomiting. Her mother was away on a trip at the time, so her father was incredibly concerned and wanted to take her to the doctor. It was then that Alexandra realized she had to tell her father what she had done. She had to tell him she was pregnant — a terrifying conversation for a teenager to have with her father.

When she told him the news, while he was very upset, he also knew that he had to try to find help, and do it cautiously. He started asking around and finally found someone willing to do an abortion for his daughter. It cost a whole month's salary. And it was something that would be, by far, the most traumatic experience in Alexandra's life.

It was November 1988. Alexandra had been instructed to go to a random address by herself, holding a bouquet of flowers. When she arrived, she entered a small room with the doctor and his assistant. She was told to lie down naked. She was shivering and frightened. No anesthesia could be used; the only thing the doctor gave her was a Tylenol. He told Alexandra that she could not make any noise because if the neighbors heard them, the police would come and arrest them all.

Alexandra tried hard to keep quiet, but the pain was unbearable and her legs moved slightly in response to it. The doctor warned her that if she moved one more time, he was not going to complete the abortion out of fear that he would perforate her uterus. Alexandra did her best to remain still, but it was impossible. Her leg spasmed again, and the doctor instantly stopped. He would not finish the abortion.

Out of desperation, her parents called a good friend of theirs who was an ob-gyn. She had just served a two-year sentence in prison for helping someone else with an abortion, so she wanted nothing to do with it. Alexandra's mother begged and pleaded. Finally the doctor agreed to prescribe antibiotics that would prevent infection and, hopefully, ensure that any remaining tissue was eliminated; that was all she could do. Thankfully, it worked, but the trauma Alexandra experienced would stay with her for the rest of her life.

Every day in Romania, desperate women were risking their lives in this way or putting their children up for adoption or placing them in orphanages because they were unable to care for them anymore. It wasn't that these parents were careless or didn't want their children. "It was poverty and feeling like there was no hope, no light at the end of the tunnel," Alexandra remarked. Either decision — abortion or adoption — was an incredibly difficult one for any woman, and that is important to understand, she said.

Hearing Alexandra's story and her experience reminded me of how easily I could have been one of the many abortion cases or how I could have been placed in an orphanage. My life could have turned out very differently — or I might not have had the chance to live a life at all.

A Startling Insight

Two years later, in 1990, Alexandra met Robert when he started to do adoption work in Romania. She had just been accepted into medical school. Alexandra said that there was no college in Romania; after high school, you would take an exam to continue on to medical school, engineering school, architecture school, or whatever professional path you wanted to pursue.

Robert frequently visited Child Protective Services to arrange the emigration paperwork for children whose adoptions he handled. It was there that he met and developed a professional relationship with Alexandra's mother. From time to time, she would extend an invitation to Robert to join her family for dinner.

It was likely that during one of these encounters, Robert said, he approached Alexandra and asked if she wanted to work for him. He needed help translating medical records, producing medical reports, and taking families to the orphanages. It offered a good source of income while she was in school, as well as the reward of helping children leave

Romania to start a better life with a family. She accepted and continued to advance in medical school and work with Robert for nine years.

I told Alexandra that my circumstances were slightly unusual: a private adoption at the age of two, after living in a village outside of Arad, in a house with my birth mother, and never being in an orphanage. Her response was a bit alarming.

"So, that means they sold you for money," she casually said.

I paused for a second before asking, "Why do you say that?"

Alexandra explained that, at the time, it was a common practice to sell a child for money in Romania. Many adoptive families did not directly *buy a child*, but cash still exchanged hands. It was "under-the-table money," so to speak. It was something that could not be stated outright — that would be against the law — but it happened all the time.

I needed a minute to process this. It was a lot to take in, and it definitely caught me off guard. Nonetheless, I was intrigued by what Alexandra said, and I wanted to look into it further. I did some online searches and found some jarring headlines:

"Romania lifts lid on babies for sale racket"
"The Romanian Baby Bazaar"
"Doctor Acts to Heal Romania's Wound of
  Baby Trafficking"
"The Baby Business"

The list went on and on. There is a pretty disturbing number of articles relating to corrupt adoption cases, as well as accusations that children were being sold and that child trafficking took place. In fact, in 2001 CNN reported that Romania had banned international adoptions because of criticism from the European Union that it was "selling children."

Seeing all of this for the first time was unsettling, to say the least. It made me think of how bad the poverty must have been if some people were going to the unimaginable extreme of putting a price tag on a child. I am not saying that was part of my story, nor am I saying that it occurred in all adoption cases, but I do believe that it happened.

"Somewhere along the line, every parent wanted some money," Alexandra said. "Even if their kids were in orphanages, if the parents hadn't signed their rights away to the orphanage, they tried to find ways to get money out of it. It's not that people were greedy. They needed money to survive."

At the same time, getting anything legalized or acquiring a piece of paper from the court also required making payments "under the table." She explained, "In a corrupt communist system, things do not work as advertised. You pay off everyone."

After 1989, things didn't change much, because corruption was part of the culture. Alexandra said that even today people in Romania take tips and bribes. Doctors, politicians, policemen, judges, you name it.

But at that time, "The expectation was that adoptive families — whether they were Romanian, American, German — gave the child's family something. Usually it was money."

I was curious what my mother's reaction would be to all of this. So, I raised the question, "Did you ever give any money or anything to my birth mother at the time of my adoption?" My parents were pretty straitlaced, by-the-book kind of people, so chances are they did not, but I wanted to ask anyway.

Marcy was quick to respond, "No, absolutely not," with no hesitation in her voice. (But would she really admit this to me even if it did happen?) The response was pretty much what I was expecting.

But she was very aware of the corruption that went on in Romania, even though it was not something she had emphasized. And she reminded me that it was the reason she and my father brought very little with them when meeting my birth mother for the first time. They did not want to risk anything being perceived as corrupt.

I believed her. But even if they did decide to give my birth mother some money, would it really have made a difference in the grand scheme of things? I was still getting the opportunity to live in the United States and reap the benefits of no longer living in poverty. I was getting the chance to have a more prosperous life.

What if there was no expectation and a birth mother did not ask for anything, but out of pure generosity an adoptive parent decided to give something to her? Is that considered "buying" the child? Why would it be?

If I am being completely honest, I don't know what I would have done in that situation. Suppose I were adopting a child in a foreign country and I saw a mother struggling to survive — a mother begging for money on the street to put food on the table. A mother who has no running water in her home, no toilet, or other basic things we take for granted every day. Why wouldn't I want to try to help her? I am not saying I would have given her a wad of money, but maybe I would have seen to it that she got some things that she needed.

To this day there are a lot of negative misconceptions relating to adoptions in Romania, stemming from this period in history. I appreciated Alexandra's transparency and her authenticity. I wasn't looking for sugarcoating. I wanted to know the truth, and she shared with me what life was really like from her perspective.

I could have easily been abandoned or just dropped off at the local orphanage, but that was not my story. I truly believe my birth mother wanted a better life for me and this was why she chose to put me up for adoption. An opportunity to dig deeper into my adoption and find out why she made this choice would soon present itself.

CHAPTER FIVE

The Search

Robert had told me, if and when the time came that I wanted to search for my birth mother, he knew someone living in Romania who could help me. His name was Daniel Musteata. Daniel and Robert had met when they were both working the adoption scene back in 1990s Romania. Robert described him as a trustworthy, good person.

In 28 years, I had never given a "search" any thought, so my first instinct was to reject it. The idea of actually seeking out my birth mother seemed like a pretty big leap. At the time, I did not think I had any interest.

It did get me thinking, though: *Why has it never crossed my mind before?* I believe one reason was that I always imagined my birth mother was no longer alive. I vaguely remember having a conversation with my parents when I was younger and them implying how unbearably hard the living conditions were in Romania. While they never said my birth mother was dead (not that they would know either way), the inference was that it was very likely that she was no longer alive. I never dwelled on it; it became something I just accepted.

The reality is that, in those days, Romania was essentially a third-world country. The living conditions were brutal, and the possibility of her not being alive anymore was a realistic one.

Later that night, I shared the conversation I had with Robert with my husband, Marc. His eyes widened with excitement at the thought of me being able to track down my birth mother. "What if she is alive?!...Don't you want to know?...Don't you want to see if she looks like you?... You might actually be able to talk to her?!" Marc's string of questions, loaded with curiosity, got me thinking more about it and the possibilities.

After all, I had already opened a can of worms, as my dad would say. I had tracked down Robert and I was now invested. I wanted to learn more about my adoption, the people involved, the process. So, how could I not go that extra step and see if my birth mother was still alive?

I could even have the opportunity to get answers directly from the source, and that began to intrigue me. Robert was handing the possibility to me on a silver platter — how could I turn it down? It wasn't long before I realized I had to do it, I *wanted* to fully commit and immerse myself in this journey so that I would have a clearer picture of my life.

The First Tentative Step

I found myself emailing Daniel to find a time to talk on the phone, to learn more about him and what the search process would be like. It was July 17, 2019, when I spoke to him for the first time. I called him after I dropped off my daughter at daycare. I made a pitstop at Starbucks before my Orangetheory Fitness class, sat on a bench outside, and dialed his number.

Daniel had a friendly voice, his English was good, and he seemed happy to speak to me. I told him a little bit about myself and explained that I was writing a book. He was curious as to why I was writing a book and why I wanted to do this search. I told him I hoped my story would inspire others who are adopted to learn more about *their* story.

Daniel told me that he had coordinated many birth family searches before and most of them were successful. But it was important to understand there was a chance he would not be able to find her — and of course, if he *did* find her, there was no guarantee that she would want to speak to him and relive the painful memory of the adoption. Daniel wanted to be very upfront about this. Of course, I understood the risks involved before I spoke to him. But I appreciated his honesty and decency. It made him seem even more trustworthy. Although I had never met Robert in person, I trusted him — so if he was connecting me to Daniel, I already knew he was reliable.

When I asked Daniel why he does these searches on the side in addition to a full-time job managing a carpet store and having a family, he answered, "I love to see how people's lives have changed. The ability to pass along information to the biological families is a powerful thing. I did adoption work for 20 years, and being able to reconnect people to their biological families is very satisfying." He was very genuine and easy to talk to. I believed that he really did get satisfaction from doing this work; I imagine that most people would.

Daniel told me these searches typically took about a month. He had some contacts who were social workers and other types of officials who could give him some guidance on how to find my biological mother. It also helped that he was familiar with the area where I was born and where she would still likely be. As we talked some more, I also mentioned there was a possibility that my birth mother belonged to the Roma (Gypsy) community, but this hadn't been confirmed.

Daniel said he had time to get started on this project as soon as I was ready to pull the trigger. After I thought about it some more, I found myself reaching out to him two days later to give the go-ahead. He told me to share with him whatever documents, photos, and information I had. He also said I should provide a letter that he could translate for my biological mother, including whatever questions I wanted him to ask in the event that he was able to find her and speak to her.

I searched the few documents and photos that I had, and found a name and an address. Who knew whether the address was still accurate, though? But it was a starting point, at least. My birth mother's name was Daniela Cirpaci. When I was born, she lived in the village of Covăsânț, in Arad County. There was a street address, and it stated on my medical records that she was 26 when she had me, which would make her around 56 today.

I don't know why really, but I thought she would have been younger. I suppose in my head, I imagined a teenage mother struggling to care for a child, leading her to put me up for adoption. That is a pretty foolish assumption given that adoptions happen at all different ages and stages of life. Regardless of her age, it had still been an incredibly difficult time to live in Romania. But that was the story I had constructed in my head, so seeing her age came as a bit of a surprise.

I thought of some straightforward questions to ask her if the opportunity presented itself and crafted a letter for Daniel to translate:

Dear Daniela,

I hope this letter finds you well. My name is Yael Adler. You put me up for adoption in 1991, when I was two-years-old and went by the name Adriana. First and foremost, I want to thank you for the decision that you made. I know that it could not have been an easy one. However, your decision is what allowed me to have a wonderful life with a loving family, and I am so grateful.

I recently turned 30 and have been giving my adoption some thought, more so now than ever before. I have a husband and two daughters. I have a full-time job and am in good health.

I would love to learn more about my adoption, and I wanted to know if you would be so kind as to answer some questions that only you have the answers to. It seemed like a unique circumstance that I was adopted at the age of two and still living in your home.

What was the reason you put me up for adoption?
Why did you wait until I was 2?
What was the process of putting me up for adoption?
Do I have any siblings?
Do you know who my biological father is?

I have no ill feelings of any kind. Anything you can share with me would be so much appreciated. Thank you for your time listening to this letter, and I hope you and your family are well.

Best,
Yael Adler

I also had some photos of Daniela and her mother, as well as of Robert and some people who worked with him, all of which I shared with Daniel.

Now there was nothing left to do on my end but wait and see what the outcome was. At night I would lie in bed and have a steady stream of questions run through my head. *Could she still be alive? Will she speak to Daniel? Will she answer all of my questions? What if I have a sibling who I never knew about all these years?*

Waiting is always the hardest part, but it was all out of my hands now. I was trusting a virtual stranger — someone I had never met in person — to get these answers.

Daniel was prompt in his initial response, texting to let me know that he received all of the documents and photos, and he was going to begin collecting information and doing research on his end. He mentioned that if my family roots are tied to the Roma people (and we were confident that they were, based on the last name), this could be a positive thing. In Daniel's experience, the Roma people have been very welcoming and willing to talk to him. So, chances were that if Daniela *was* still alive, there was a strong possibility that she would speak to him. This was reassuring.

Daniel was very good at keeping me in the loop and letting me know where he was in the process and who he had been communicating with. Each time I heard from him via text was thrilling, not knowing what new piece of information I would learn.

And fairly quickly, in a matter of just weeks, it was revealed that Daniela was alive!

Wow, I thought, *this is something I really need to wrap my head around. My birth mother is actually alive.* It was a strange thing to imagine. All these years I thought she was deceased, and I had been wrong. She is alive, and Daniel found out where she lives. He had everything he needed now to make the trip from Braşov, where he lived, to Şepreuş, the village where Daniela was now living.

This was getting exciting but kind of crazy. I had to pinch myself a couple of times to remind myself that this was actually happening.

I tried to put myself in Daniela's place for a second. Picture one day just going about your daily routine when suddenly there is a knock on your door, and it is this stranger asking you about the child you put up for adoption 28 years ago. What a bomb to drop on someone! That moment would very likely change her life forever.

I don't know if I would have the courage to do what Daniel was doing. So, I sure was relieved that I had him doing all of the heavy lifting for me. And soon, the weekend was finally here — the weekend that Daniel was planning to go see Daniela. It was a long drive for him, about seven hours one way. All I could do was wait by my phone.

Saturday, August 26, 2019

It was 7:00 a.m. when I woke up. My older daughter had gotten me up a couple of times in the middle of the night because of a bad dream, so Marc let me sleep in a little. I must have grabbed my phone to check if I had heard anything from Daniel since Romania was seven hours ahead of New Jersey timewise. The phone was still in my hand when I awoke. My eyes widened. I had a text from Daniel!

Oh, my God, I thought, this is it! What is he going to say?? I took a deep breath and opened the message. It said, "I am with Daniela, she would like to speak to you."

Did I read that correctly? I had to look at the text again to make sure I had it right. Yes, that is what it said. He was actually with her! I could not believe it.

But was I ready to talk to her? I was definitely not expecting this. I called Marc, who was downstairs with the girls. He ran up to see what was going on.

"Marc, Daniel is with my birth mother right now and they want to FaceTime."

"What?! Oh, my God, I have to go get dressed and wash up." He rushed to the bathroom.

I laughed. *YOU have to go get ready?* I thought.

I was not prepared for this. In my head I pictured that Daniel was going to find her, talk to her, and then he would just send me a report with everything I wanted to know. I didn't really think ahead to the possibility that she might want to speak to me. I rushed to put on some makeup and at the very least a decent shirt with my pajama pants. I went to the corner of my room where there was a little sitting area, and I texted Daniel "Ok."

I tried to pretend that I wasn't nervous, but how could I not be? For the first time, I was going to see the woman who gave birth to me. But what was I going to say? I did not have a chance to really collect my thoughts. This completely threw me off guard. I am a planner; I like to plan things ahead of time and organize my thoughts. I was freaking out and slightly nauseous, but I took another deep breath and the next thing I knew, my phone was ringing.

I hit "Accept."

I saw Daniel come on first. He was smiling. It was my first time seeing him. He had dark brown hair, fair skin, bushy eyebrows, and an oval face. If I had to guess, he was probably in his 40s. Daniel happily said, "Hello Yael, I am here with Daniela," and slowly panned the phone so that she was in the frame.

Suddenly I saw this woman with a round face and black hair pulled back, smiling at me. She was not wearing any makeup. She wore a white and royal blue striped t-shirt with flowers on it, and behind her was a gate and some trees. She was obviously sitting outside her home.

It felt like I was in a movie. Stuff like this doesn't just happen every day in real life. I wasn't sure what Daniel and Daniela had already talked about privately, so I did not even know where to begin. Thankfully, she had questions for me. She wanted to know about my life. About my kids, my job, my husband. I had Marc sitting next to me, whispering questions to me, which was helpful because it seemed I couldn't find any words. I really just wanted to stare at her and see what similarities we had. I was trying to take it all in. I could see her clearly, but obviously it wasn't the same as seeing someone in person.

At first, it was difficult to feel an emotional connection. For starters, I was not prepared for this type of meeting. Our conversation was being orchestrated by a translator since we did not speak the same language, so it was hard not being able to speak to her directly.

She introduced me and Marc to her husband, whom she'd been married to since 1997. His name was Vosu (pronounced "Osho"). He had a kind smile and wore a short-sleeved blue button-down shirt. He was tall with a protruding belly. The first thing he said was "You are very pretty." We laughed. This was the first man Daniela had a relationship with since my adoption in 1991.

Marc chimed in from time to time and asked questions. I was glad because it was difficult for me to think clearly. Daniela's demeanor was pleasant. All I wanted to do was study her and get a sense of her personality (or as much as I could get through FaceTime). It was probably going to be the only time I would get to see her, I thought.

She said she hoped that I was not upset with her. I tried to reassure her that I had no ill feelings and that I was so grateful to her for giving me such a good life, which was the reason I wanted to find her — to thank her.

I asked if she would like to meet my daughters. She nodded her head with excitement and said yes. When I had both of my daughters come into the room, her face shone with joy. She blessed us all many times and said how happy she was that we were all in good health. You could tell that she was a good person.

Towards the end of our conversation, she asked if I would be willing to visit her as long as it was okay with my mother and family. Surprisingly, I didn't hesitate: I told her that I would like to visit. I wasn't sure *when*, but I would let her know. She was happy to hear this. Immediately after I thought, *Why did I say that? Did I mean it? Or was I just being polite?* I wasn't really sure.

Daniel had a long trip back home, and the poor guy was sweating from the heat outside (you could see the beads of perspiration on his forehead), so it felt like it was time to end the call. It seemed like a successful conversation; we had covered a lot except for some of the big, obvious questions that I had asked in my letter, which Daniel said they already covered. So, we said our goodbyes and thanked Daniel for making this possible.

When we got off the phone, Marc and I looked at each other. We were both just blown away at what had happened. I kept waiting to feel something, but I didn't. I just felt like I was talking to a stranger. Marc had gotten more emotional during the conversation than I did. I thought, there has to be something wrong with me. I just spoke to the woman who gave birth to me and put me up for adoption 28 years ago, and I didn't *feel* anything? No tears, no sadness, no happiness, nothing. Maybe I just needed time to process everything.

Then I thought about Daniela. How on earth can she go on with her day after what had just happened? I wish I knew what was going through her head.

I thought about what I had said. *What if I did go to Romania to visit her in person?* Without a doubt, that would be much more satisfying. The adventure was appealing, and seeing her in person would be so different than just doing a FaceTime call. Then I could also see where she lived and where I was born. It would be a completely different experience.

I ran the idea by Marc, to see what he thought. He was immediately on board and thought it would be a good idea to take the trip. We just needed to figure out the logistics of it all, with our busy work schedules and looking after our kids.

I was going to give it some more thought and see if it made sense. In the meantime, I was beyond eager to see the report that Daniel was going to write up for me. After all, I still did not have answers to anything relating to my adoption. In part, I think that was also why I felt slightly unsatisfied. While it was nice having the chance to see my birth mother, it felt incomplete without those answers.

I would have the report soon, and there it would be all laid out in front of me. I waited for that email, refreshing my inbox frequently every day, waiting.

CHAPTER SIX

The Report and Its Aftermath

The day finally came when, on October 19, 2019, I got the email from Daniel with the report he had prepared, promising all of the answers to my questions. I was anxious to open it. It was kind of exciting not knowing what I was going to learn. With one click, I would be able to read about a part of my life I never knew before, and the thought of this was both exhilarating and terrifying. I opened the attachment.

I could tell that Daniel had put a lot of thought into the report. Not only did he prepare it on a nice stationery template but it began with a warm, personal note saying how grateful he was to be a part of this journey. Daniel commended me for my bravery in the steps that I took to conduct the search and reminded me how not all adoptions are successful, nor do the searches always have a happy ending.

I was fortunate to have both be true in my case. It *did* have a happy ending, which is what drove me to write this book and share my story in the first place. And the search was successful. Not only was Daniela alive, but she was willing to share her story and share key information about my adoption.

The report covered personal information about my biological family and explained the rationale behind my adoption. I am referred to as Adriana, which was my Romanian birth name. The following is what Daniel shared with me.

Personal facts about the biological mother, father, and sister:
Fact 1

I, Daniel Musteata, personally established contact with the biological mother, Daniela Cirpaci, her married name now Hrista, of Șepreuș, Arad, on August 26, 2019. Daniela Cirpaci was born in Curtici, Arad, in the family of Traian and Floare Cirpaci. Birth date June 12, 1962. Daniela has been married to Vosu Hrista since June 24, 1997, according to the marriage license issued by Covăsânț, Arad, authorities. Officially she has taken the name of her husband, Hrista. The couple does not have children together and currently lives in the village of Șepreuș, Arad County, with Floare Cirpaci (Daniela's mother, who is approximately 90 years old).

Daniela has one other daughter, and her name is Monica Covaci. Monica is married to Remus Covaci. They live in Simand, Arad, with their own children. Monica was born on April 29, 1986. She has two daughters, Adryana (18) and Estera (10), as well as two boys, Benjamin (13) and David (17). I could not establish personal contact while visiting Daniela, but I spoke on the phone with Monica. She has a Facebook account and desires to connect with her sister since she has learned about her. Daniela spoke to Monica about her sister only after I visited.

Monica was born from a different biological father, and she has no relationship with him. However, she stays in touch with her mother. When Monica was a child, she went to school only until the fourth grade. She knew her husband at the age of 14, and the two moved into the house of the husband. This is typical in

Gypsy families: At an early age, the family of the boy looks for a wife, and around age 12 to16 the children get married while continuing to live under the same roof as the boy's parents.

Regarding your biological father, Fanica, Daniela could not give any information except that he was two years younger than her, and he was not a family man. He did not come to see her at the maternity hospital after the birth of Adriana (you), and he used to be violent and abuse alcohol. The relationship stopped before the birth of Adriana, and Daniela raised the two daughters with the help of extended family.

Daniela and her family belong to the ethnic group known as Roma or Gypsies. The Roma (*Roma* in the Romani language, *Romi* or *Ţigani* in Romanian) constitute one of the largest minorities in Romania. According to the 2002 census, they number 535,250 people or 2.5 percent of the total population, being the second-largest ethnic minority in Romania after Hungarians.

The Roma are, however, Romania's most socially and economically disadvantaged minority. Many Roma people do not have an identity card or birth certificate. Since 2007, many members of this ethnic group have migrated to Ireland, Spain, France, Belgium, and Italy.

Place of birth and circumstances of adoption: Fact 2

Adriana was born in the maternity hospital in Arad as the second child of Daniela Cirpaci. The biological mother was in a relationship with Fanica, hoping to form a family, while she had another child (Monica) with a different man, who did not assume family responsibilities. In the beginning Fanica seemed to be a good match, but he did not keep it up. Daniela's expectations to have the support of a man to raise children did not turn out as she hoped. Before Adriana was born, Fanica abandoned Daniela and did not have any interest in her or the daughters.

Daniela was living in the village of Covăsânţ, Arad, in a small house consisting of a single room and a porch where other relatives shared space. The house had electricity but did not have running water, and the conditions for raising two children were not appropriate. Daniela was very poor, and she was suffering from back pains. At the time of Adriana's birth, Daniela did not want to abandon the baby, and she brought her home to raise and care for her. With no support from a man while abandoned with two daughters, Daniela's life was more and more difficult every day. She was working occasionally, helping people in the community for food or small amounts of money, while caring for Monica and Adriana and hoping for a change in the relationship with Fanica. However, he didn't show any interest in her or the daughters.

Although Daniela is one of six sisters and one brother in her family, everyone had their own difficulties and could not offer much support. Daniela did not go to school, as her parents did not consider education important for the children. Social and political circumstances were very different at the time when Adriana was born, compared to how the country later changed as it progressed to democracy.

Romania was on the verge of a public revolt when baby Adriana was born. In December 1989 a revolution broke out, which led to the collapse of communism and execution of the dictator Nicolae Ceauşescu. He had banned contraception and abortion in Romania, and by the time his regime fell, almost 100,000 abandoned children were living in neglect in homes and institutions across the country. Up to a third of those children eventually found new homes. There were so many babies born into poverty in Romania, and their parents couldn't afford to keep them.

Many couples in the West offered to adopt children after programs about their plight were broadcast on television. It was during this time that Mr. Robert Braun started to adopt children out of Romania, initially from poor families and a few years later, when the child welfare system became more organized and adoptions were allowed only from public or private institutions, through the accredited agencies.

What was the process? Why was the adoption from the house at the age of two?
Fact 3

Pediatricians or social workers together with lawyers often knew where a single mother or a poor family was struggling with raising children. Along with an adoption facilitator from abroad, they would visit the house of such people and offer to help with identifying a family who would adopt the needy child. According to Daniela's declaration, she was told that if she would consent to the adoption, a loving family would come to adopt Adriana into a foreign country and the baby would have a much better life.

She gave some thought to this for a few weeks and the next time someone asked what she wanted to do with the baby, Daniela asked that person if he knew where the baby would go. She was told the baby would go to America! At that time, America was the best place a person could hope to go: the dream land. Then she asked if she would be able to know who would adopt, and she was told the family would visit her.

Because Daniela could not care any longer for two daughters, she gave her consent and the adoption process started. This decision was very difficult, and people in the village were divided; while some supported her in this decision, many others judged her. The mentality was that you could not be certain what would happen after the adoption is finalized. Would this family be honest people who want to care for a child in need or would they be human traffickers who would exploit the child?

Despite all this, Daniela hoped for the best, that this facilitator and the adoptive family would be honest people, and she took all the judgment of the community upon herself. The foreign facilitator and other people visited her with the adopting family, assured Daniela of all their support, and told her this adoption is in the best interest of the baby. While she was troubled because she couldn't offer her children the life they deserve and with the pressure of the community at the alternative of adoption, Daniela took courage and made the decision, thinking that this family would give the baby a better life, one that she could never offer.

Thus, when the time came, she went before a judge at the courthouse in Arad and consented to the adoption with full effects of filiation of baby Adriana. The adopting family told her that when they would be able in the future, they would come to see her again, but since that moment she did not know anything of the baby until the very day when I visited her with the letter from Adriana. During the intervening years, Daniela hoped and prayed for the baby to be well, and awaited the day when the adoptive family would let her know anything about her daughter.

As the years passed, she could not speak to anybody about her burden and the mixed feelings of hope and regret buried inside her heart. Most people who knew what happened were judging her, and only a few supported her. During all this time she did not speak with anybody about what happened, because she thought that people could not understand her, what is in her heart, nor the circumstances that forced her to make this decision.

Despite the difficulties, she as a single mother continued to raise Monica, the older daughter, on her own after the adoption of Adriana. Daniela never wanted to have her children in a childcare institution. This is the reason Adriana was adopted privately and not from an orphanage. Regarding the age when the adoption was processed, there is no other reason this happed at two years except that it was when Romania was free from the communist regime and foreign people were able to come into the country. Until that time, Daniela had both children in her care and made efforts to raise them while also caring for her mother, who was ill. Daniela did not have any other relationship with any man until she met Vosu, whom she married in June 1997. The couple couldn't have children of their own.

When she married, Daniela moved from the village of Covăsânț, where she had her daughters, and continued her life with her husband, Vosu, in the village Şepreuş. The house the family has is decent-looking, larger than the house in Covăsânț, and made up of three rooms, a porch, and a yard. The house is connected to electricity and has a well for water. The mother, who is approximately 90 years, lives with them and Daniela takes care of her.

Since the borders opened and people can freely travel into the European Union, from time to time Daniela is able to go out for limited periods to make money for the family by working in France. She cannot speak the French language, but she goes abroad into Roma communities.

Warm Regards,
Daniel

So Much to Consider

I read this report many times. Each time I read it, my heart went out to Daniela for what she had to go through. Two abusive relationships, no money, trying to care for two children on her own, in a house that didn't even have running water.

Without even meeting Daniela in person, I knew she was a strong woman. I knew that she wanted me to have a better life — and because of her, I did.

I pictured the scrutiny she had to endure. The judgment, the stares. The burden of having to live with this decision every day in such a close-knit community, with no outlet to vent or release her stress. Her heartache.

I was surprised to see how many siblings Daniela had. I wondered what her mother's reaction was to the adoption. This woman birthed and raised seven children by herself! Times were even more difficult when Daniela and her siblings were children. Was her mother disappointed in her? Or was she understanding? My hope is that she was a shoulder to lean on and that some of Daniela's family, if not all, gave her some support during that difficult time.

To think that, all of these years, I had a sister only three years older than me, us living completely opposite lives. I was surprised to see that her daughter's name was Adryana, which seemed like a pretty wild coincidence, even though Monica did not know about me. I was very curious about this and hoped that one day I would have the opportunity to ask her about it.

I gave some thought to Monica's upbringing and how she lived in a culture where being an only child was a rarity. She grew up around family and friends who most likely had multiple siblings, and she was led to believe that she was an only child. I imagined that the loneliness she probably felt, well beyond the typical lonesome feelings of an only child, must have been difficult for her.

I grew up as an only child, too. Sure, there were times when I was lonely and wished I had a sibling, but I don't think it affected me in the same way that it probably affected Monica. I knew other only children, and while it was less common, being an only child certainly wasn't something that greatly impacted my life. But it would have been really nice to have an older sister growing up. To think, if I never did this search, I never would have known about Monica. This further fueled my desire to travel to Romania, so I could meet her.

When Daniel mentioned in the report that she was on Facebook, I started searching for her. I must have messaged ten different Monica Covacis in Romania, asking if they had a mother named Daniela, but I never got a response. Finally, one day I posted something on my Facebook page and one of the "Monicas" left a comment with a smile emoji. I remember thinking, *Oh my God, that's my sister!* I was so happy to find "my" Monica Covaci, and from that point on, we became friends on Facebook.

I got the chance to see a photo of her, which was pretty exciting. However, it was hard to see what she really looked like, because she only had one photo and it was of her and her daughter with a funny photo filter with oversized glasses. But from what I could see, we both had a round face, brown hair, and almond-shaped eyes. I am sure if we were to stand side by side, people would believe that we were sisters. And the thought of getting the chance to meet her in person and actually stand next to each other was sort of mind-boggling.

The idea of going there had been growing in my mind for a while now. I knew Marc would be okay with it; he was very supportive of me wanting to explore this part of my life. He had already said that I should go, that it would be "the trip of a lifetime," which is definitely true.

No, Marc wasn't the issue. How would I tell my mother? THAT would be a difficult conversation. She was fully aware of me wanting to write a book and my conversations with

Robert, but this? She would never in a million years expect this.

It would be difficult for her. We are talking about the woman who got teary-eyed every time I brought up the subject of my adoption. Not that I blame her for that — I mean, she could have made an effort to be slightly more approachable, but then it had always been a very emotional topic for her, as it would be for many people.

Telling my mother about this trip was something I was looking to postpone for as long as possible. I decided I would hold off telling her until the details were final. Why get her all worked up about something that might not happen? *Once I have a flight booked, I will tell her,* I thought.

CHAPTER SEVEN

My Romanian Journey

Preparing For The Trip

On November 6, 2019, I booked my flight to Romania for December 4. I would leave from Newark, New Jersey, have a layover in Munich, Germany, and then arrive in Timişoara, Romania. This airport was a lot closer to Arad, which is where I would be staying, as opposed to flying into the capital, Bucharest. After it was all booked, it still felt slightly surreal, but the reality of actually making this trip was starting to kick in.

I had come a long way from first finding Daniela to FaceTiming with her, but I was unsatisfied with the ability to connect with her given the lack of in-person interaction, the language barrier, and the need for a translator to guide the conversation. It wasn't until I began shopping for gifts two weeks before my trip that I started to feel anxious. Shopping for gifts around the holidays can drive anyone crazy, but this was different. I felt like there were so many people I had to get gifts for, and I didn't know what to get because I didn't *know* any of them; they were all strangers to me. I can't tell you how many times I Googled "gifts to bring Romanians from the US" or filled up my Amazon Prime shopping cart with a bunch of crap and then deleted everything, just to do the same thing all over again.

I was obviously overanalyzing what to get everyone, but I couldn't help thinking of all of the people involved. I would be meeting my birth mother, Daniela, my sister, Monica, and her four children, Daniela and Monica's husbands, other relatives — and of course, Daniel. Without him, this trip would not even be possible. There is no way I would be able to get around Romania by myself without speaking the language or knowing the lay of the land. I was so grateful that he was taking time off from work and away from his family to do this for me.

I kept picturing a scenario of me showing up at Daniela's house and a whole village of people there awaiting my arrival. I began feeling overwhelmed. I texted Robert and told him that I was starting to feel a little stressed out, and he responded with some sound advice.

"In every musical, there is a director and a choreographer. You are the director here, and Danny is the choreographer," he said. "You need to be more in control of the arrangements if that would make you less anxious." Robert was right. He suggested that rather than going to Daniela's house for the first meeting, we should meet somewhere neutral — a café or the hotel, where we could meet privately but it would still be more personal than FaceTime. I would have more control over the situation, and then we could always go back to her house later that day if that felt like a natural next step.

Robert was so helpful; he really put things into perspective for me and calmed my nerves. When I told Daniel how I was feeling, he was also very understanding and took care of all the arrangements.

My husband suggested I put together a photo album for Daniela — an idea that I loved. It would be something she could always have to look at. After all of those years of not knowing if I was happy, healthy, and living a good life, it would reassure her that her decision was a good one. I could finally show her a glimpse of my life and how it has been filled with so much joy over the years. I was looking forward to doing this for her.

Daniela had been through so much hardship and scrutiny from her community for the decision to put me up for adoption. She suffered for the two years raising me on her own with no help and hardly any resources. She gave me the opportunity to go to the place other people only dreamed about.

Breaking The News

My nerves were slowly building as the trip drew closer. There were still so many unknowns and for a control freak like me, that was a difficult pill to swallow. Typically, I like to know what is coming so I can prepare myself. Aside from the airfare and hotel arrangements, Daniel had done all of the coordinating and communicating with Daniela and Monica. I had no clue what the itinerary was, who would be present, nothing. I was basically traveling blindly to a foreign country where I didn't speak the language, taking a once-in-a-lifetime chance, and hoping for the best.

There was also the fact that I still needed to tell my mother all of this. I knew I had to rip the bandage off and talk to her about it, so I thought carefully about how to approach it. I arrived at the conclusion that I would call her therapist to ask if she could facilitate the conversation and help my mother process this news I was going to tell her. Perhaps this was the easy way out, but nonetheless it would be incredibly helpful.

Of course, the therapist agreed, so we planned to talk during her next session.

"Mom, there is something I want to tell you."

"Ok, what is it?"

"Well, you know how I am writing a book about my adoption?"

"Yeah."

"Remember I told you I was hiring someone to do a search for me to see if my birth mother is alive?

"Yeah…" I could tell by the tone of her voice that she was growing wary of where this conversation was heading.

"Well, I found out that she is still alive, and that I actually have a sister whose name is Monica."

"Okay . . ." She knew there was more coming.

"I have been giving it some thought, and I am going to take a trip there to meet them and see where I was born."

"What??…" There was a tightness and some fear in her voice now.

Phew. It was a huge relief getting this all off my chest. Then the crying started, and my mother was confused, not understanding why I would want to do this. She kept asking, "I am still your mother, right?"

I wasn't really sure what she meant. *Of course, she is my mother! I know I dropped some major bombs on her in one conversation, but what does she think — I am going to pick up and move to Romania and never see her again?!* Well, she probably did feel that way.

Thankfully, the therapist was there to help my mother look at the situation from a different perspective, and we were able to leave the conversation in a better place. I explained to my mother that this was just something I was interested in exploring. She is, and will always be, my mother. I just wanted to be able to see where I was born and learn more about my adoption. Fortunately, she understood and accepted my decision to take this trip. And I promised her that I would speak to her every day I was there and that everything would be okay.

The Trip

Before I knew it, December 4 was here and I was ready to embark on my journey to Romania. I got up that Wednesday morning, worked out, got a blowout, and threw on some light gray sweatpants with a loose black sweater so that I could be comfortable on the plane. As luck would have it, there was a mix-up with the mail and the beautiful photo album I had created online to bring with me for Daniela got delayed and never made it with me on the plane. I had called UPS nonstop, verbally abusing every agent I spoke to, and each person told me a different story, but they were all consistent in saying that I would get the package before I left. Well, that didn't happen, so I had no choice but to accept it. I would have to explain this to Daniela and figure out a way to get the album to her.

I took an Uber to the airport and struck up a conversation with the driver. We spoke about traveling abroad, and he told me about an upcoming trip he would be taking to India for a family wedding. Taking my mind off my own trip relaxed me. I was tired, and I hadn't eaten anything. Truth be told, I was looking forward to sleeping on the long flight. When you have little kids, you tend to appreciate two things more and more: quiet and sleep.

I arrived at the airport, checked my bag, and made it through security pretty quickly. I had some time to kill, so I found a restaurant near my gate and ordered a glass of cabernet and a steak sandwich to try and relax a little before my first flight, which was eight-and-a-half-hours long. I sat at the bar, hoping everything would be on time and that the flight would be smooth. I was not a fan of flying.

After I ate, I remembered that now I had no gift for Daniela. I could not go empty-handed, so I went into one of the duty-free shops and bought her a bottle of Tiffany perfume and a box of Godiva chocolates with the Statue of Liberty illustrated on the box. Perfume is a tricky thing to buy someone, I know, but I figured even if she didn't like the scent, the bottle was pretty and it would look nice on her dresser. I pictured her looking at it and thinking of me.

Before I knew it, my plane was beginning to board. I had gotten a window seat, in the hopes of passing out on the long flight — which of course did not happen. I ended up watching some movies and occasionally drifting off. At least there was only a young girl to the right of me, and she did not take up much space. She wore her headphones the whole time.

We arrived in Munich around 7:30 a.m., and I had four hours to wait before my connecting flight. Munich has a pretty amazing airport; if you are stuck with a few hours to kill, this is a good place to be. There are tons of shopping options, from high-end luxury designers like Burberry, Gucci, and Bottega Vanetta, to other shops with gourmet chocolates and great gifts. The restaurants and cafés all looked incredible, and I even passed a section containing "napcabs," where people could rent an enclosed space to sleep a little in between flights. I thought that was pretty cool.

I did not have much of an appetite. My whole schedule was thrown off, given the time difference and the lack of sleep on the first flight. So, I just ordered a cappuccino and a small pretzel sandwich with lox and spread on it. I didn't really want it, but I forced myself to eat because it would have been sinful to pass up the delectable food showcased all around me.

I went to the gift shop and bought a bunch of tins of different chocolates and snacks to bring home with me. Even though I would be returning to this airport on the way back, I would only have a 45-minute connection, so I knew I wouldn't have any time to shop. After I bought more gifts, I headed to my gate to charge my phone before the next flight.

As the airline called passengers to board for Timişoara, I headed into the jet bridge thinking it was taking me to the inside cabin of the airplane. In reality it took me outside to where we had to take a shuttle to an isolated lot where our plane was waiting. I thought, *Where the hell is this taking us?* We were then dropped off right in front of the plane, with airstairs leading us inside. This was very different than what I was used to. But I guess when you travel to random destinations like Timişoara, that is what happens.

I napped on this short flight and woke up to the pilot's voice announcing our descent into Timişoara. When I looked out the window, the sky was clear and there was a lot of greenery. Mostly fields with small pockets of houses. I took a deep breath. *I am really here,* I thought.

We soon landed in front of the small airport with capital letters at the top saying TIMIŞOARA. I got off the plane hoping that I would not have trouble finding my way around and meeting up with Daniel. As I went through security, the woman who looked at my passport showed it to the colleague next to her and chuckled. I am not sure what was so funny. Maybe it was the fact that my passport says I was born in Romania? Who knows. As I continued, I was relieved to see there was only one baggage carousel. *No way I could get lost here!* I thought. I spotted Daniel right away in the crowd, awaiting my arrival. *Thank God.* Everything was off to a smooth start.

We had never met before, but we had been talking for months, all leading to this "reunion," as Danny called it. (He insisted I call him "Danny" instead of "Daniel.") I already felt very comfortable around him, plus Robert spoke very highly of him. We greeted each other with a hug, and he helped me with my luggage. I couldn't have asked for better weather in December. It was around 40 degrees Fahrenheit, the sun was out, not a cloud in the sky. It was the perfect day to walk around and explore. I wasn't that tired because I had slept most of the last flight, which was 90 minutes long. I was feeling refreshed and eager to sightsee.

We got into Danny's car and drove to Piaţa Timişoara, which was the center of town. It was very charming, with cobblestone streets, beautiful buildings and churches which have been restored or were in the process of being restored. They all had a pop of color to them, and the architecture was stunning. I could just imagine what a popular spot it must be in the warmer months, with outdoor cafés and plenty of scenic sitting areas.

That weekend, people were celebrating St. Nicholas Day, an Orthodox Romanian holiday in honor of St. Nicholas, who would come on the night between December 5 and December 6 with gifts for children who have been good; those who have been bad receive sticks instead as a punishment. It has become a tradition to decorate sticks around this holiday, and as we walked around the town, we saw many kiosks with vendors selling food and these ornate sticks with different embellishments on them.

We stopped at a café where I ordered a coffee. I was looking forward to a nice big cup of fresh brewed coffee after my flights. The woman handed me a tiny cup and then read the surprised look on my face. She asked, "Would you like some more hot water with that?" I thought she was giving me a sample to try but then quickly realized that she gave me espresso, which is what everyone in Romania drinks. Danny laughed, knowing that what I was expecting and what I actually received were two very different things. We picked out some pastries to share and sat down at a table.

Danny and I drank our coffees and spoke briefly about the adoption work he used to do. He was telling me how, around 1997, he started his own agency to help families adopt children in Romania. Once the country no longer allowed international adoptions, he had to make a career change. Today he manages a carpet store; they install carpets in churches and all kinds of commercial venues.

After we chatted for a little bit, Danny and I decided to head to Arad, where we would be staying. It was about an hour's drive. We arrived at the Hotel Continental Forum Arad; it was clean and modern, and seemed like a touristy kind of hotel. After we checked in, I went to my room to unpack and freshen up for dinner. The room was a nice size, with a red theme throughout and a good view of the town center.

Later, Danny and I met downstairs and walked outside to find a place to eat. The temperature had dropped a lot, and I needed my gloves and scarf. I kept telling Danny that I wanted to try good, authentic Romanian food, so we started walking to a place where he remembered having a nice meal on a previous visit. Unfortunately, when we got there, we found that it had gone out of business. Luckily, there was another place next door, and the food was great.

My first Romanian meal consisted of *sarmale*, which are stuffed cabbage rolls filled with meat. We had *sarmale* with cheese-topped *polenta* and sour cream on the side, which you are supposed to mix together; it was very creamy and delicious. We also shared sausage and a beef stew with some more *polenta* (*polenta* is super popular in Romania, if you haven't figured that out). I am not sure that a vegetarian could survive in this country, but as a foodie who eats everything, I enjoyed every bite.

There was a big family next to us celebrating their daughter's first haircut, which apparently is a tradition that people celebrate. Danny talked me into ordering *ţuică*, a traditional Romanian distilled brandy made from plums. People typically consume it before a meal; it is served in a shot-sized glass and meant to be sipped. I thought I was drinking gasoline; it was so strong. I took one taste and could not endure any more. Danny laughed and said that Robert was not a huge fan of the drink either.

After our meal we left the restaurant and walked back toward our hotel, where there was another outdoor market with vendors selling food and other things. It was there that I got to experience *kürtoskalács,* also known as chimney cake. This is a Hungarian sweet bread that is made on a grill on a large skewer and then placed in a long bag so you can enjoy breaking off pieces and unraveling it. *Kürtoskalács* was amazing. We also had some warm sangria, which I'd never had before; it was very sweet but hit the spot.

It had been a long day of traveling, so after we got our sugar fix, we walked back to the hotel to rest up for the big day when I would meet everyone in my birth family for the first time. They would be coming to the hotel, where there was a nice restaurant in which we could sit at a quiet table and get to know one another. In only two full days, I planned to meet everyone, see the hospital where I was born and the courthouse where my adoption was finalized, and learn about the culture and my roots. It was a lot to cram in, but I was feeling excited, nervous, and so many other ambivalent emotions.

CHAPTER EIGHT

Day One – The Reunion

Friday, December 6, 2019

I woke up around 6:00 a.m., feeling a little groggy from the seven-hour time difference. I tried to go back to sleep, but thinking about the day ahead made that impossible. At around 8:00, I decided to just get up, wash up, do my makeup, and put on something nice that would be my "first impression" outfit. Everything had gotten creased in my suitcase and there was no iron in the room, so I had asked the front desk if they could have all my tops dry cleaned the night before. I wanted to look my best. I chose a light gray sweater with embellished sleeves and black leggings with my knee-high black suede boots that had pearl-trimmed low heels.

Danny was already waiting for me downstairs, where they served a complimentary breakfast. I went down to meet him, feeling like there was a knot in my stomach. Normally I would still be sleeping at this time, so I was not hungry. I made my way over to the coffee machine and fixed myself a cappuccino. I was getting tense knowing that in about three hours, Daniela and Monica would be coming to the hotel. I tried to just breathe and relax the best I could, but I did not know what to expect.

Danny went over a few things at breakfast, saying that he wanted me to feel prepared (as if that were possible). He told me first off that Daniela and Monica would be coming with their husbands and Monica's four children. In my head, I had pictured it just being Monica and Daniela for the initial meeting, so now it went from three to nine people! (Including Danny.) *That is a lot of people all at once*, I thought.

Next, he told me more about Daniela. He said that from time to time she travels to France to clean houses and beg for money. "She begs for money?" I repeated back to him. That was difficult to even say out loud. I was shocked to hear this, and my heart was flooded with sadness.

A part of me wondered why Daniel even told me this. Did he want me to sympathize? Did he want me to give her money? Or did he just want me to understand her life? I wasn't sure.

After breakfast, we thought it would be nice to get some photos printed from my phone for everyone to look at since my photo album never made it on the trip. Luckily, right across the street from the hotel, there was a photo store where I could get the photos printed. I also bought two mini photo frames, planning to take a photo to leave behind with Daniela and Monica. I had brought with me an Instax Mini camera, which prints photos on the spot for you. The camera had been a birthday gift for my four-year-old daughter, borrowed for this occasion.

After we got everything, Danny and I walked back to the hotel. I went up to my room and of course, changed my outfit again, as if it mattered what shirt I was wearing. I met Danny downstairs, and we headed to the restaurant in the hotel to ask them to set aside a table for all ten of us. Initially Danny proposed that I wait up in the room until they arrived and then come down to join them, but the notion of making some grand entrance with eight strangers plus Danny staring at me seemed terrifying. I asked Danny if he minded just sitting at the table in the restaurant and waiting for them there, even if it meant sitting for a while. Fortunately, he was very easygoing and was okay with whatever made me more comfortable. So that is what we did. Danny and I sat and waited.

I thought it might be polite to have some appetizers on the table when they arrived. Just as I was placing the order, Danny said, "I think they're here." From where we were sitting, we could see a group walking up to the hotel's front entrance. They were hard to miss; there were so many of them, and they were all dressed up for the occasion, which showed how thoughtful they were. The women all held large, beautiful bouquets of red, pink, and peach roses with gold airbrushed petals.

Danny went out to greet them and bring them inside.

A funny thing about the placement of our table: there was a wall right in front of it that acted as a divider, so I couldn't actually see the family come into the restaurant. Only when they walked past this wall would I see them. It was like a big reveal.

Daniela walked in first. She rushed over to me and held my face, with tears streaming down her own face. Adriana, she said over and over. She kissed my cheeks and just kept crying. I hugged her and kept saying, "It's okay, don't cry." This sweet woman unleashed 28 years of pain, 28 years of thinking she was never going to see me again. But there I was, standing right in front of her.

Daniela was just about the same height as me, around 5'1", and was dressed all in black. She wore a black headscarf with light gray polka dots, a black long-sleeve cardigan sweater with some sequins, a long black skirt, and a pair of black dress loafers. She did not wear any makeup. She seemed tired and appeared older than she really was. I recalled our FaceTime conversation, when she referred to herself as "old" multiple times; when I told her that 56 is considered young here in the States, she found that hilarious.

Her skin was beautiful, practically flawless. Looking at her up close, I could see we definitely had a similar facial structure. We both had almond-shaped eyes, the same nose, and the same creases by our mouths. But her eyes carried a lot of pain and sadness. She did not smile. I could tell she didn't smile much.

The next person who greeted me was Monica's daughter Adryana, who at first, I thought was Monica! They looked almost identical. She was wearing a blue lace sleeveless dress and, unlike the other women there, was wearing some makeup. Next was Monica, who was so happy to meet me that I could feel her excitement in the hug she greeted me with. She was dressed conservatively, with a black blazer and a navy-blue lace dress. She also looked older than expected, although she was only three years older than me.

Then I met the rest of Monica's children — her two sons, David and Benjamin, and her other daughter, Estera. Then the husbands, Vosu and Remus. I had "met" Vosu briefly during the FaceTime encounter over the summer. As I guessed even then, he was just like a big teddy bear. The husbands wore black hats and were dressed in suits.

We all took seats at the table. I sat between Daniela and Monica. Danny sat across from me, handling all of the translation and filling in the gaps of silence. There was a lot of silence, because my mind was racing and I couldn't seem to put my thoughts into words. Daniela held my hand on her lap under the table, which strangely did not make me feel uncomfortable. My hands were a little sweaty from nerves, but I don't think it made any difference to her.

I kept telling everyone to order some food. The Jewish mother in me was kicking in, as if food were the answer to everything and would relinquish any awkwardness. I didn't know what to say to Daniela or Monica, let alone her kids! Daniela said that she could not eat anything, that her stomach could not handle any food. She kept looking at me as if she had dreamed of this moment for so long. She ran her fingers on top of my polished nails. It was as if the nail polish on my fingers showed some sign of privilege. A reminder of something that she could not give to me.

I tried to strike up a conversation with the kids. I could only imagine what Monica had told them and what was going through their heads. "Oh, hey kids, by the way, I have a sister who was put up for adoption at age two. She would have been your aunt. She is flying here from the United States, and oh yes, we will all be meeting her at her hotel." What?? The situation was hard enough for adults to wrap their head around.

I tried to keep it light and fun. In an attempt to break the ice, I asked about school, what some of their interests were, if any of them had boyfriends or girlfriends. The older son, David, was in college. According to Danny this was a pretty big deal in the Roma community for a child to go to college.

Danny seemed surprised and impressed, and spoke to Monica's husband for a few minutes on the topic of education. While they were talking, I looked over at Monica and tried to talk to her using Google Translate. Daniela was frustrated and kept saying she wished she spoke English. The feeling was mutual — I was desperately wishing I could speak their language.

Finally, everyone ordered food. Once it came out, Remus stood up to say grace before the meal, which was something they regularly did. I have no clue what he said, but you could tell that it was heartfelt. Remus seemed like he was kind and a good family man who was genuinely appreciative for this nice meal and all of us being together.

I made the mistake of ordering tripe soup—for those of you who don't know, tripe is cow stomach. It was on my list of things to try, being a traditional Romanian dish. But I literally could not get it down and was probably insulting everyone at the table by not eating it. Tripe's not bad — for me, it was a textural thing. The buttery broth was good, but I just could not swallow the rubbery bits of tripe. I didn't want to offend anyone, so I tried picking at it, but Daniela could tell right away that I was not enjoying it. She smiled and shook her head with her nose scrunched up, as if to say, "You don't like it, do you?" I think it amused her.

Danny had the server take it away, telling her I was not used to this type of soup, which made everyone chuckle. I ordered the cabbage rolls instead, knowing that was a safer choice. Changing the subject, I said that I had gifts for everyone and handed out the shopping bags. They all smiled but did not show much interest. I kind of wanted them to open their gifts so it would give us something to do, but they all just thanked me. They were not interested in anything material; they just wanted to spend time with me.

I thought it would be a good idea to circulate some of the photos I had printed, so we started passing them around. Then Monica took out her phone and, much to my surprise, showed me all of the photos she pulled from my Facebook page and saved to her phone! *Wow*, I thought. I couldn't believe that she had all of these pictures of me and my family from over the years.

I didn't really have a list of things I was looking to accomplish in this first meeting. I just wanted to take it all in and go with the flow, even if it meant there were some awkward moments.

Remus talked about his job and how he managed a farm while it was Monica's job to stay home to take care of the house and the kids. I wondered what was going through her head. I wished I knew what was going through everyone's head, but *especially* hers and Daniela's.

We continued small talk here and there. Then Daniela asked if it would be okay to go back to her house because her sister Carolina would love to meet me, but she would be leaving in the morning. We had planned to go to the house the next day, but how could we say no? So, we got the check and took some photos of everyone at the table and then some of Monica, Daniela, and me by the Christmas tree in the restaurant. Daniela did not smile in any of the photos. I had to keep telling her to smile and she would make an effort to do so for me.

I ran upstairs to get my coat and then Danny, myself, Daniela, her husband, and Estera piled into Danny's car for the trip to Daniela's house while Monica and the rest of her family took their car to meet us there. Daniela sat next to me in the back and protectively put her arm around my shoulder so I would be close to her. It felt comforting. I told her, "Let's take a selfie!" and

held out the phone so she would know what we were doing. It was then, for the first time, that I got a smile out of her, and it made me *really* happy.

The house was an hour or so from the hotel. It was getting dark and as we got closer, the roads became winding and it was definitely more remote. Daniela lived in the village of Şepreuş, and I'm not going to lie, it felt like we were in the middle of nowhere. There were no stores, no gas stations, no people in sight. We were out there, alright.

We pulled up to Daniela's home. There was a very pretty ornate gate with gold trim around the front of her house. I wished I could have seen more, but it was dark out at that point. We walked in and there was a small but lovely courtyard with hanging flowers. Then she took us to a cozy room that was painted a bright yellowish-gold color. There was a brown sectional sofa that took up most of the room, where everyone gathered around a coffee table that had a nice spread of food that Daniela had generously laid out. It consisted of flavored sodas, chicken cutlets, a salad, and homemade cabbage rolls. There was a small, freestanding fireplace that kept the room nice and warm.

Daniela's mother, Floare, was sitting at the edge of the sofa close to the fireplace. She was dressed in a black satin jacket with a black polka dot skirt, matching stockings, and a floral apron around her waist. This adorable, petite woman, at age 92, was losing her hearing and her eyesight. And yet, when I came in and they told her who I was, she took my hand to hold in the sweetest way when I sat beside her. It was like Floare remembered me.

Then I got to meet Carolina, one of Daniela's sisters, who would have been my aunt. She was so happy to see me! Carolina said my Romanian name, Adriana, with such love in her voice, as if she had been waiting years to call me that again. It felt like I was a long-lost relative who had returned home and everyone was celebrating. Carolina said she was so upset after my adoption that she named her daughter after me. I was so moved when she told me this.

It later came out that when Monica heard Carolina's daughter's name, Adriana, it resonated with her. She loved it so much that she chose it for her own daughter, with a slightly different spelling. Little did Monica know that she had named her daughter after her sister!

I was the only one eating. I felt like it was the polite thing to do, to take some food — and besides, I am a stress eater, a nervous eater, and any excuse to eat, I pretty much indulge. Everyone just watched me. Once I took a break, Monica quickly said with excitement, "Okay, now that you had some food, it's time for cake!"

At first, I didn't understand her excitement. Then Monica came back with a sheet cake with a photo of my husband, Marc, myself, and my two daughters on it! It read *Bun venit sora mea Adriana!* translating to "Welcome my sister Adriana!" They had all gone to such great lengths to make me feel welcome and a part of their family. Daniela had also made a cake, which might have been the most delicious cake I have ever had — a moist pound cake filled with layers of sweet cream and jam.

After cake, they all lined up and took turns handing me shopping bags filled with gifts for me, my daughters, and Marc. The presents were overflowing. They bought me a jacket, clothes, matching outfits and shoes for the girls, and a sweater for Marc. They really outdid themselves.

Then Daniela presented a special gift to me: a traditional Roma outfit, consisting of a pretty red floral dress, a similar red scarf for my shoulders, and a matching head scarf. We took a video of Daniela dressing me in it. I could tell it brought her a great deal of joy to see me wearing this outfit. She told me that I looked like a doll.

After that, we all sat together and chatted. Remus talked a little about Roma life and how arranged marriages are still practiced and can take place as early as age 12 or 13. I joked that I didn't think anyone would want to marry me because I don't like to cook, which made everyone laugh. Remus was quick to say, "If you were living here, you would learn to cook," which is true, I probably would. Whether I would enjoy it or not was a different story.

It was getting late, and we still had to drive to Monica's house. (Earlier, we had offered to drive her home so that the whole family would not have to cram into one car.) Her house was another hour away, so it was time to say good night to Daniela, Vosu, and Floare. We agreed to see each other again the next day at Monica's house. Monica and her older daughter, Adryana, came with Danny and me. Remus and the other children were in the other car. We followed them.

I was pretty exhausted but determined to keep the conversation going. With the language barrier, it was hard to prevent our talk from being choppy; it was all stop and go. I told Monica that I was going to ask a bunch of random questions so I could get to know her a little bit, and turned it into a game. I asked her trivial things like what her favorite foods were. Did she like Chinese? Italian? She told me that she never had Chinese food, which makes sense — that type of cuisine is not very common in Romania — but she said she liked pizza. Adryana chimed in that sometimes she makes it from scratch at home. I told them I could live on pizza every night if I knew it wouldn't make me gain so much weight. They laughed.

Then I moved away from the lighter questions and asked Monica what it was like hearing about me for the first time. She said she was just so happy to learn that she had a sister.

We arrived at Monica's house, which looked nice from the outside and had some signs of life surrounding it. While Daniela lived in a very remote village, here there were some small convenience stores and other places nearby. We all said good night and that we looked forward to seeing each other again tomorrow.

Danny and I had about another hour's drive back to our hotel. It had been a long day, and we were both worn out. I had not slept well the night before, so I was looking forward to a hot shower and a good night's rest. We got back to the hotel and told each other that we would meet downstairs for breakfast. I got back to my room, checked in with Marc to see how the girls were doing, and then fell asleep shortly after, feeling more at ease and looking forward to seeing everyone again the next day.

CHAPTER NINE

Day Two – An Intense Experience

Saturday, December 7, 2019

I was so tired the night before that I hadn't bothered to set an alarm. So, when I woke up the next morning it was around 10:00 a.m.! I jumped up, not knowing if Danny had planned to leave at a certain time. I texted to let him know that I had just gotten up and would start getting ready to meet him downstairs in half an hour.

I washed up, did my makeup and got dressed, making sure to put on the jacket the family had bought for me. Downstairs, I headed right to my cappuccino machine to have some coffee. I looked at the breakfast spread this time and decided on marinated mushrooms and eggs over easy. It was definitely more of an Americanized breakfast, but they still had some traditional Romanian meats and cheeses.

As Danny and I sat and ate, he told me we would head to Monica's house for a short visit. Then he would show me around Arad and some places he thought I would like to see, such as the maternity hospital where I was born, the courthouse where my adoption was finalized, an orphanage, and sites relating to my adoption. Danny also knew that I wanted to do some shopping so I could bring gifts back for family and friends.

I was getting a little nervous about seeing everyone again. With the communication challenges, I tried thinking of things I could say to them. I ended up watching a YouTube video with some common Romani phrases, thinking I could surprise them when I walked in. Romani is not an easy language (I felt like I could pick up Romanian quicker), but I just wanted to practice some phrases for fun. Danny and I ended up listening to the video on the car ride to Monica's. One phrase seemed manageable: "How is everything?" or "How's it going?" which was *Sar san*. When we arrived and I saw Daniela eagerly waiting for me, I repeated this one phrase to her, making an effort to connect, which I think she appreciated and found amusing at the same time.

Daniela walked me inside and took me to the dining area, where everyone was sitting at a large rectangular table. I spotted Remus wearing one of Marc's basketball t-shirts that I had brought for the boys, which I thought was pretty funny. It was a little snug, but it was nice that he was wearing it. Monica's house was more spacious than Daniela's and had gold trim everywhere. Of course, on the table was a nice spread of food, consisting of kebobs of meats, cheeses, and olives.

They were ready to treat me like a guest of honor all over again. Monica offered me some coffee, which was good and much needed. (I was having some serious Starbucks withdrawal and was still adjusting to the time difference.) After we had coffee together, I asked if Monica could show me around her home. Monica and Daniela were happy to take me on a little tour. Each child had their own bedroom and there were small, flat-screen televisions around the house. The backyard was very nice, with a simple pool and emerald green arborvitae-like trees around the perimeter of the yard. It was very scenic and pretty.

I asked Monica if I could use her bathroom, so she showed me where it was. Daniela was waiting for me right outside the door as I came out. She pointed to the toilet and said, "Toilet, me no toilet" with her finger moving back and forth. *Did she just tell me that she did not have a toilet? No, I told myself, I must have misunderstood.*

We rejoined the group back in the dining room and sat for a little while to chat some more. I was saying thank you for having me and welcoming me into your home, and they were all saying how happy they were to have me there with them and that I was "family."

The next thing I knew, Monica and her daughter Adryana were bringing out several pizza pies for lunch, to surprise me. They knew I really liked pizza based on the conversation we had the night before. All of a sudden, I started to cry. Once again, they were going out of their way to do all of these thoughtful things for me to make me feel special. I was overwhelmed by their kindness and the love they showed for me.

After we ate, I sat with Daniela and we listened to the Romani YouTube video I had played in the car. I wanted to show her that I was attempting to learn some phrases. She could not read or write, but since they said the phrases out loud in the video, it was something we could do together.

The day was getting away from us, so I told Danny, "Why don't we take some photos and then say goodbye?" We went outside and took a lot of pictures with everyone. Then I took individual shots with Daniela and Monica. I put the photos in the frames I had bought for them.

As we were getting ready to go, Daniela started getting very emotional and upset. She knew I was leaving the next day, and this was not sitting well with her. It was then that I learned she had a heart condition, so it was not in her best interest to get worked up. Daniela also hadn't eaten much since I arrived. Monica pulled out a chair for her to sit down. *Oh God, please do not have a heart attack,* I thought.

Daniela started saying things to Danny like "I regret my decision" and "I wasn't in the right mindset." Monica was getting worried. She was saying things to Daniela, Daniela was saying things to Danny, and here I was in the middle of it all, not knowing what the hell anyone was saying! I just felt the intensity of it all, and it made me extremely uncomfortable and worried. I felt terrible that I was the cause of Daniela's pain.

Tears were streaming down her face as she called my name over and over again. *Adriana. Adriana.* Danny looked at me and said with a sense of urgency, "We need to go, now."

I didn't know what to do, so I followed his lead. We all said goodbye one more time, and gave hugs and kisses to one another. Danny and I headed toward the car. We smiled and waved from inside as the family gathered around.

Once we were alone in the car, I asked Danny if it was possible that Daniela did not have a toilet, and he told me yes, it was very possible. There were many people living in rural areas who did not have indoor toilets. Danny said they just go to the bathroom "outside." That really upset me.

I thought this would be the last time I was going to see them before my flight, but then Danny told me that they all planned to make the trip to the airport the next day to see me one last time.

"They are?" I asked in surprise.

Danny said, "Yes," with a smile, knowing how much they wanted to spend every last second with me. In a way, I was conflicted about it, seeing how upset Daniela got today. I wondered if it would be worse for her to come to the airport the following day and have to say goodbye all over again. It was so kind of them to want to go out of their way, and travel two hours there and back, just to see me off. I could tell that was something they did for family without any hesitation.

More Unexpected Gifts

As we drove, I became less tense and was looking forward to seeing some of the sights. Our first stop was Arad, where we found parking on the congested narrow streets and landed right in front of the courthouse. It was a pretty, beige three-story building with white columns and capital gold letters across it that read *PALATUL JUSTITIEI*. As I stood in front of the courthouse and had my photo taken, I imagined what that day must have been like for my parents. I pictured them walking in thinking, "The day we have been waiting for has finally come!" knowing that they were only steps away from having a family.

The next stop was the maternity hospital of Arad, the place where I was born. I could not walk up to it like the courthouse because there was a fence around the perimeter of the building. But from a distance, I saw the large, white building with many square framed windows. And as I looked at it, I pictured Daniela going into labor and holding me for the first time. I could see her looking at me with a lot of love in her heart, the same way she had looked at me many times on this trip. I could only imagine the level of stress she was under when she had me, thinking of having to raise two children on her own. I wondered if the stress she felt outweighed the happiness and what was going through her head when she took me home that day.

Next, we went to the Child Protective Services building and then an orphanage. The orphanage was undergoing construction or was being shut down — we weren't sure which — so it was vacant and looked pretty rundown. Danny shared that he remembered visiting this orphanage and spending many hours in the courtyard playing with children and getting to know them in hopes of finding them a family. I imagine it must have been strange for him to come back after so many years had passed.

It was a reminder that the orphanage could have easily been part of my story, and then who knows how my life would have turned out. I was so grateful to Daniela for not putting me in an institution like this and for choosing to give me a better life. It was a pretty cool experience, getting the opportunity to physically visit all of these places that were relevant to my adoption. It truly was a once-in-a-lifetime trip.

After the orphanage, we headed back to the car and decided it was time to go shopping. First, we approached a mall and pulled into the parking garage, which was dark and looked kind of creepy. Danny and I both felt like something was off, which was confirmed when we went in and realized the entire mall was closed.

"Way to take me shopping," I told Danny.

We laughed, and Danny joked, "You can see how long it has been since I was here." We went back to the car to try again and ended up at the Atrium Mall, which was colorful and full of people. It was big and had pretty much everything you could want or need: grocery stores, appliance stores, and other shops that are typically independent stores here in the States. But hey, it was certainly convenient having everything all in one place.

Danny and I went into a gift shop, where I bought a couple of decorative bottles of Romanian wine for family and some holiday cards in Romanian for Robert. I picked up some "Frozen" and "Fancy Nancy" coloring books in Romanian for my daughters and my nieces, and was on a mission to find really good Romanian snacks and treats to bring back for my sister-in-law, who is a total foodie like me. As we went inside the grocery store and walked down each aisle, I told Danny to point out all the good stuff and tell me what I should get. We were dumping chocolates and cakes and gummies and chips into the cart. I'm pretty sure we got something from every aisle, but it all looked good and was pretty reasonably priced, so I went a little nuts.

Once my wallet felt a little lighter and we had several full bags to carry back to the car, I realized that the day had flown by and it was already dinnertime. We were passing the food court and decided to grab something quick since we were both tired, and I had lots of packing to do. As we were walking through the food court, I spotted a woman in a bright green and gold trimmed dress and a head scarf. Danny pointed out that she was a *Gypsy* woman. I thought, *Well, she definitely stands out in the crowd,* and I supposed that was the point.

It was interesting to watch her and then see her join her family, walking in a straight line with her husband at the front of the line, her children behind him, and then her at the back. It is customary for the Roma people to walk like this in public, Danny explained.

We ended up having chicken gyros for dinner. I was hoping to have more traditional food, but I was too tired to care. We were going to try to spend some time in Timișoara in the morning, where I was planning to stop by a festival and eat some authentic food before my flight. We ended our meal with some gelato and headed back to the parking garage.

I felt like I had accomplished everything I wanted to on this trip. I got to meet Daniela, Monica, and their families for the first time. I got to see where I was born and learn a little about the culture and traditions I was born into. I got to eat delicious Romanian food. I got gifts to bring back home with me, and now I was ready to go home. I missed my girls, Marc, my house.

When we got to the hotel, I thanked Danny for being such an amazing tour guide, translator, and person. He really *made* this trip, and without him it would not have been possible. I gave him gifts for his daughters and for the newborn he was expecting. We hugged and said goodnight.

Packing, I knew, was going to be interesting. I was well over the weight limit and had already accepted that I was going to have to pay a fee. Getting everything inside and zipping up the suitcase was another story. When I arrived, my suitcase had been filled with gifts, and leaving for home it was once again filled with gifts. I had not expected the amount of generosity that Daniela, Monica, and their family showed me. It was far above and beyond anything I could imagine. Yet somehow, I managed to get it all packed up.

Then something else unexpected happened. I started getting random friend requests and messages on Facebook, one after another. Word was getting out fast that the long-lost Adriana was in Romania. Some of these messages just said, "Hi, I am your cousin"; some did a hand wave emoji (they didn't speak English) while others were more heartfelt. One in particular stood out:

12/7/19

"Hi, my name is Angela, or as our family calls me, Gina. I am your cousin. I am so happy to see you have finally found your mom. I used to hear the stories of you and wonder when I'll ever see you, but thank God we have found you. Everything happens for a reason, and it's all part of God's plan. I live in Ireland. I'm here since I was very young, but I hope to meet you face to face one day. Take care and God bless."

I was so taken aback. It was crazy to think that my visit was spreading to the entire extended family. It was a surprise, but it was also flattering to know that all of these people wanted to introduce themselves to me and get to know me. It was also refreshing to interact with some people who spoke English.

It was all so surreal. This trip, the culture, the communication with people contacting me out of the blue. It was hard to sleep that night. When I closed my eyes, I pictured Daniela. I couldn't help but feel like a huge disruption in her life. I had awakened a lot of feelings and memories that were so painful for her. I know she was happy to meet me and spend time with me, but seeing how upset she was made me feel heartbroken. It felt like my presence was hurting her in some way, and that was the last thing I wanted.

I worried that saying goodbye at the airport was going to be very difficult for her, and I almost wished that she wouldn't put herself through it all again. But I also knew that nothing was going to stop her from coming, and there was something sweet about that. I wished I was able to speak the language and get to know her and her family better. I felt like they did so many nice things for me and I did not have a chance to do much for them. I thought about some final words I wanted to say to them before leaving and wrote a little note for each one of them on my phone, which I would read and have Danny translate at the airport.

Monica,

I wish I could have spent more time with you. I would have liked the chance to do more nice things for you after everything you have done for me. I would have loved to have a "girls' day" and be sisters: eat Chinese food, take you to get your hair and nails done, and just have fun.

But in many ways what we did do together was more special. You welcomed me into your home, into your family, and into your heart. The way you showed me so much love made me feel like we really are sisters. In the little time we spent together, it is so clear to me that you are a good person and a wonderful mother who did a great job raising four beautiful children who are so lucky to have you. I may be far away, but you will be in my thoughts and you will be close to my heart.

Let's keep in touch on Facebook and continue to share photos and be involved in each other's lives.

Remus, [Monica's husband]

Thank you for all of your kindness. It has been such a pleasure meeting you. Please take good care of Monica. I wish you nothing but good health and happiness.

Vosu, [Daniela's husband]

Please do me a favor and take good care of Daniela. All I want is for her to smile and to feel happiness in her life. I have enjoyed our time together, thank you for showing me so much love.

Daniela,

Words cannot express how grateful I am and will always be for the life you have given me. Having the chance to meet you and spend time with you after 28 years has been so incredibly rewarding and special. I have really enjoyed our time together, and I will never forget all of the love and the warmth you have shown me on this trip.

You are a strong woman who has experienced much hardship. My heart goes out to you, thinking of everything that you have been through. I want you to know that you will always have a place in my heart and that I wish you nothing but good health and happiness. This is not goodbye; we will find a way to keep in touch through Monica, and some day in the future I will see you again.

Until then, you will be in my thoughts.
- Adriana

Sunday, December 8, 2019

The next day, Daniela, Monica, and their husbands did come to the airport to see me off, and even Adryana came along to say goodbye one last time. Thankfully, my worries proved to be unfounded. While Daniela and her family were sad to see me go, we were all just happy to be together and to soak up all the details of the last few minutes of our visit.

After I read the family members their notes (with Danny's help, of course), they gave me yet more gifts to bring home. We had to take things out of my suitcase and rearrange it several times, but we made it work. We hugged and said our final goodbyes as I approached Security.

There was so much to think about, so much to process. I was just so happy that I took a chance. A chance to meet everyone, to learn more about my adoption, and to fill in the missing blanks.

I felt ready to return home, to my life, to my family. But I would never forget about my Romanian family. They were part of me now.

CHAPTER TEN

My Roma Roots

I felt so blessed to have met everyone and to discover what kindhearted, welcoming people they were. It was eye-opening to see how they lived in the rural villages of Romania and to hear stories of their traditions and culture.

After my trip, I felt a sense of guilt reflecting back on a conversation I had with Robert long before conducting this search. When he first introduced the word *Roma* to me, I asked him what it meant. He said, "Gypsy."

Gypsy? I repeated it back to him with a tone of disapproval and surprise in my voice. Yes, he said. "That is not a dirty word, you know." He told me some of the coolest and most gracious people he has encountered over the years have been a part of the Roma community.

I suppose I responded that way because all I ever knew about Gypsies was how they were portrayed cinematically: as poor, thieving, nomadic people with a flamboyant appearance. Obviously, if these are the things you associate with the word *Gypsy*, you wouldn't exactly be thrilled about it. And I had never met anyone who was Roma. They are certainly not a common sight in Morris County, New Jersey, where I live.

But I recognized that I was a part of the problem. The first thought that entered my head was negative images of Gypsies, which led to me drawing a conclusion without even knowing anything about them. Too many people share that same ignorance, and the media needs to stop fueling it by depicting Gypsies in negative and stereotypical ways.

When discussing the title for this book, I could tell some people were hesitant to embrace the word *Gypsy* under the belief that it is offensive. I took that feedback constructively and wanted to research the issue some more. I asked my sister, Monica, and another relative what they thought of the word, and got somewhat surprising feedback: they both told me it is not the word itself that is offensive — in fact, many are proud to call themselves *Gypsy*. It is only when people use it in a derogatory context that it becomes offensive. That made me realize there is a huge misconception out there that needs to be addressed. *Gypsy* is not a negative word.

On EachOther, a human rights non-profit website, I came across an article called "I'm a Gypsy — I Want My Grandchildren to Be Proud of That Fact." It featured Sherrie Smith, a Gypsy activist who said, "I say 'Gypsy' because there's a lot of beliefs that that word isn't liked by us anymore — it is." (Source: EachOther website)

Unfortunately, the challenge that women like Smith are looking to overcome is that some people are afraid of what others will think of them because they are Gypsy. In addition, some people have engaged in negative behavior that has tarnished their reputation. Because of this, many Roma have faced an immense amount of discrimination; their children get bullied and there are hate crimes against this group of people simply because they are Gypsy. In response, Smith developed Report Racism GRT (reportracismgrt.com), which is the first online platform for reporting hate crimes against Gypsy, Roma, and Traveller communities.

With all of that being said, when I learned that I was born a Gypsy, it added a whole new dimension to my adoption, because it was an aspect that I never knew about. It was unique enough that I was born in a foreign country like Romania, but now I learned that I was born into a community that was even more culturally different.

So, what have I learned about the Roma people? What are some of their customs, their culture, and their traditions? Through some online research and conversations with my family in Romania, here is some of what I have uncovered:

10 Quick Facts About Roma People

- This ethnic group goes by several different names, including Rom, Romani, and Roma.
- It is believed that the Roma people originated in northern India.
- Their language is called Romani; some say it has similarities to the Punjabi and Hindi languages.
- Today, Roma live in different parts of the world, but large populations live in Europe, in countries including but not limited to Romania, Bulgaria, Serbia, and Hungary.
- While they belong to different social classes, many are socially and economically disadvantaged.
- Rom means "man" or "husband."
- Arranged marriages are still common today.
- Up until a few years ago, most Romani children stayed at home without any formal education, although this is evolving as education becomes more highly valued.
- The majority of Eastern European Roma are Roman Catholic, Orthodox Christian, or Muslim, but they are also known not to follow a single faith.
- Family is an integral part of Roma life.

Imagining What Might Have Been

I couldn't help but think about how drastically different my life would have been had I grown up with Monica. As early as age 12, I might have had an arranged marriage. My parents would have been in communication with a boy's family, and they would have determined if we were "a match." I would have lived with my in-laws until we had children — who knows how many, maybe four kids, maybe six. (The Roma all have pretty large families.) Then my job would primarily have been to tend to the household, raise the children, cook, go to church, and spend time with family.

I would have had little to no education and possibly not known how to write or read. I would not have had a chance to experience grade school, high school, or college. I would not have gotten the chance to learn about my interests, my skills, my passions. That all would have been nonexistent. But that would have been my life, and I wouldn't have known anything different.

I would have lived in a male-dominant society. And while this does not apply to all Roma men, many of them are known to abuse alcohol and women. It was heartbreaking to learn that Daniela was subject to two abusive relationships — men who physically beat her while she tried to take care of Monica and while she was pregnant with me. It made me wonder, *what would my fate have been? Would I have ended up like the many Roma women who got beaten?* It is a definite possibility.

The worst part is that these women have no way out and no place to go for help. There is no access to therapy, shelters, and other resources in the villages like we have available to us here in the United States. Where can they go? What can they do with their children? Either they are stuck in an abusive relationship or maybe they have a chance to run away or the husband might abandon them.

When Daniela learned that I was coming to visit her, she asked if my husband, Marc, would be joining me. I told her no, he needed to stay back home to look after the kids when they are not at school, so that I could come. She was very troubled by this and worried: If I went somewhere without Marc, would it upset him? Would it be detrimental to our marriage if he was the one staying home looking after the children? I tried to reassure her that our marriage would still be intact when I returned. The glaring cultural differences were strong, and while some of the questions that came up initially amused me, these are very real issues to Roma women.

Another thing I learned was that Roma women rarely travel without their husbands. Even when Daniela travels to France to try and make money, Vosu travels with her. Now, I love my husband, but if I had to spend every second with him and did not have any time by myself or time alone with friends, I would surely go insane. But that is how Roma life is. The Roma marriage dynamic is very different, and the women usually need permission from their husbands to do things. The wives do not speak openly and freely in their husbands' presence; they tend to be more reserved and let the husbands speak first.

While Roma communities have modernized a great deal and have come a long way today, I have to think about what it was like nearly 30 years ago and what the realities of what my life would have been to highlight how grateful I am: I had the opportunity to go to school, to find a job that I love, to marry who I chose to marry, and to have an amount of independence that I never would have had. Daniela made that possible by making the decision to put me up for adoption.

With so many differences, I wondered if there are any similarities between us. Giving it some thought and through research, it occurred to me that we do have some things in common. For starters, being Jewish and belonging to a minority group, I am familiar with being discriminated against, as many still are. Historically speaking, Jews were not the only ones executed in concentration camps during the Holocaust; in fact, the Roma people were also targeted, and an estimated 400,000 Roma were killed by the Nazis. (Source: Britannica)

At the time of my adoption, my parents did not fully disclose that they were Jewish, due to a fear that the adoption might be denied because of anti-Semitism, which was still prevalent in many countries then. There are also many stereotypes that exist among both our groups which affect public perception. The main difference is that today, Jewish people have come a long way and have been more accepted and intertwined into society (in some places more than others). Being Jewish does not interfere with getting an education, getting a respectable job, or thriving in a community, whereas being Roma can make that difficult.

It troubles me to think about the inequalities the Roma have to face every day. It is their sense of family and strong community that keeps them going. With family having such importance, I think about how impossible Daniela's life must have been to even consider adoption. The amount of physical pain, stress, and poverty that must have consumed her. Was she viewed as someone who turned her back on family? Did she get any support? She had to carry the burden of her decision every day. That could not have been easy.

No amount of words could ever truly capture the sense of gratitude I will always have for Daniela giving me this life. I was so glad I had the opportunity to meet her. Flying 22 hours round-trip by plane to look her in the eyes and say thank you was the least I could do.

CHAPTER ELEVEN

Homecoming

I never anticipated how much Daniela and Monica would both be so ingrained into my thoughts in the weeks and months after I returned home. I guess I thought I would go there, meet everyone, and it would be a special trip, but I would feel fulfilled upon returning home to my life and move on. Only it wasn't like that.

I kept replaying certain parts of my trip over and over again in my head. For instance, I could not accept that Daniela did not have a toilet. I became fixated on it and thinking about how I could somehow arrange for her to get one. I didn't care what it would take, I knew I had to get her one. It didn't seem right. *Here I am living this great life, and she doesn't even have a toilet.*

How is it that 28 years later, her life is still so hard? Sure, she found a non-abusive husband and moved into a bigger home. Don't get me wrong, those are two substantial life changes. But she was still financially strapped to the point where she needed to travel to France to beg for money.

The woman who gave me up for adoption so that I could have a better life *begs for money*. That thought destroyed me inside. I wanted to help her. In messaging Monica, I told her that I wished I could help Daniela get a toilet. Daniela told Monica to tell me not to worry about her. That she would be fine. From what her family expressed, Daniela does not ask them for help; she is used to doing things on her own.

As her birthday approached in June, I made arrangements with Danny to do some research and get Daniela a toilet. I know a toilet may not seem like the most glamorous birthday gift, but I could not go another minute knowing that she had to go outside when she needed to go to the bathroom. Monica promised that she would take Daniela to pick out a toilet and send me a picture once they had it. I was never so excited to see a picture of a commode in my life; the thought that this might improve her life in some way brought me joy.

There was so much more about Daniela that I wanted to know. She had some nieces who spoke English who had already reached out to me. We chatted from time to time through Facebook, so I thought I would ask about Daniela and see what they would say. One niece told me this:

Her life has been more suffering than good times. As I know her, she can't get stressed because of her heart. If she gets angry, let her say what she has to because if you don't, she will get a knot in her heart and collapse. That is what we have been told.

What I love about her is that she will stand between men and talk. She gave me hope that women can be something more in this world. When I was small, she was very wise — like I said, only men are allowed to make decisions and talk, but she is a leader. She doesn't know how to read or write, but she has life lessons.

She has been through a lot. She is a role model to me. (I haven't said that to anyone before.) She had no other way, it wasn't that she wanted to give you away, she loved you. My mom used to take care of you and do your hair and be there for the family when Daniela had to get injections in her spinal cord. My mom went to people and picked fruit and vegetables to bring home food and help pay for the injections.

My mom told me that after you left, for months the house was like someone died. They were all mourning and crying. It was very hard for them all, and now to know that you are back in their lives — it's a miracle because they thought they would never see you again.

I will never understand the magnitude of the pain Daniela felt when giving me up for adoption. But this note showed that she was such a strong woman. It seemed like she possessed a lot of admirable qualities, and I was so glad I had the chance to meet her.

It sounded like the whole family was deeply affected by her decision. While I was there, I couldn't help but feel like they all felt sorry for me to some extent, thinking that I felt unloved or wanted. But truthfully, my mind never went to that place. I only feel grateful for the life that I have, and I hope Daniela knows that.

Monica and I write to each other every day. Most mornings, I wake up to a picture of a cup of coffee with a message saying, "Good morning sister, how are you today?" or "Good morning sister, let's have coffee." We use Google Translate to communicate back and forth. I think we both enjoy using the word *sister* in almost every sentence. Like we are making up for lost time. It is still strange to think that all of these years, neither of us knew that the other existed.

Monica always goes out of her way to tell me how much she and Daniela love me. I will never forget when she said, "Now I don't feel so alone anymore," knowing that I exist. Those words really stuck with me.

She told me that since Daniela has met me, she feels regret for her decision but is still so happy that I found her. Monica said if only she was older and understood what was going on, she would have spoken up and not have let Daniela put me up for adoption. "I am sorry, my dear sister, for all that has happened, and I apologize on behalf of Daniela. I thank God that he put it in your heart to look for us," she said.

I told her that there is no reason to feel bad about what happened. Daniela had a difficult life, and she made the best decision for me. I have a great life here, and I am glad Daniela made this choice. It seemed like Monica felt some misplaced sense of guilt, but she was only five and did not know what was going on. I think what she was really saying is that it would have been nice to have a sister growing up. And I agree, it would have been nice. But she feels like a sister to me more and more each day anyway. We send pictures to one another, and at times when someone is available to translate, we video chat. I know we will always make the effort to be a part of each other's life, no matter the distance between us.

I really believe that I was meant to search for Daniela, and I was meant to meet her and Monica and connect with them. I was meant to see what my life could have been like; I just wish that Daniela could see what my life is like here. I think that would give me the ultimate satisfaction.

I presented Daniela and Monica with the idea of visiting me here in the United States, which excited them, but the process involves a lot of moving parts. They would need to apply for visas and go for an interview in Bucharest, which is on the opposite side of the country. Then there is the challenge of getting around the airport and through customs not knowing how to speak English. We kept trying to find a relative of theirs who spoke English and could accompany them, but it did not seem like anyone would be able to make the trip.

Then COVID-19 brought all plans to a halt and ended any thought of traveling anywhere anytime soon. It was crazy to think that only a few short months before, I had taken the trip to Romania. Timing is everything.

Someday in the near future, I will make arrangements for Daniela and Monica to visit me so they can see my life here. Then this journey will have gone full circle — and I will know that Daniela truly understands that her decision was a good one.

First-time author Yael Adler wrote *From Gypsy to Jersey* to share her uplifting personal story, in the hopes of inspiring and helping other adoptees who want to learn more about their past. She has a bachelor's degree in journalism from the University of Arizona and is currently director of marketing for Sage Thrive, a company that implements mental health support services for public school districts. Married, the mother of two girls and currently expecting their third child, Yael and her family live in New Jersey.

Yael can be reached by email at:
yaeladler31@gmail.com

ACKNOWLEDGEMENTS

I am so grateful to a number of people who made this book possible. I would like to thank Robert Braun for always making himself available to answer all of my questions and connecting me to the incredible sources who were instrumental to my search and my story. They all guided me along the path of discovery that allowed me to uncover the many mysteries of my adoption.

I would like to thank Daniel Musteata for being such a kind-hearted person who devotes the time to conducting birth family searches. Without him, I never would have been able to learn about my roots or had the chance to meet my birth family and see where I was born.

Daniela Cirpaci and Monica Covaci, thank you for welcoming me into your homes and hearts, and wanting me to be a part of your life. You have shown me so much love, and I am so happy that I was able to find you.

Thank you to Carla E. Huelsenbeck and Catherine Gigante-Brown for your wonderful editing skills, and to Vinnie Corbo for believing in my story and welcoming me into the Volossal Publishing family.

Finally, I would like to acknowledge my parents, my husband, and my whole family for being so supportive of this journey and my book.

Disclaimer

Portions of this book are told from the recollection of individuals and from their personal points of view. Certain names and identifying characteristics have been changed.

CPSIA information can be obtained
at www.ICGtesting.com
Printed in the USA
LVHW011955241020
669606LV00013BA/900

9 781735 018423